monsoonbooks

PATTAYA UNDERCOVER

Ewe Paik Leong is a member of International Thriller Writers in Eureka, CA, USA. His novel *A China Doll in KL* and non-fiction works *Kuala Lumpur Undercover II, Penang Undercover* and *Pattaya Undercover* were nominated for the POPULAR-The Star Readers' Choice Award in 2013, 2018, 2019 and 2020 respectively. *Saigon Undercover* is his fifth book in the bestselling Undercover series. His food reviews and travel articles have also been published in the Malaysian print media. Ewe divides his time between Bangkok and Kuala Lumpur, where his family lives.

Other books by the author

A China Doll in KL
Kuala Lumpur Undercover
Kuala Lumpur Undercover II
Pattaya Undercover
Penang Undercover

Saigon Undercover

EWE PAIK LEONG

monsoon

monsoonbooks

First published in 2021
by Monsoon Books Ltd
www.monsoonbooks.co.uk

No.1 The Lodge, Burrough Court, Burrough on the Hill,
Leicestershire LE14 2QS, UK.

ISBN (paperback): 978-1-912049-90-5
ISBN (ebook): 978-1-912049-91-2

Cover design by Cover Kitchen.

A Cataloguing-in-Publication data record is available from the British
Library.

Printed and bound in Great Britain by Clays Ltd, Elcograf S.p.A.
23 22 21   1 2 3 4 5

Contents

Saigon Dolls

"For a male, you come to Bui Vien Street as a boy, and you leave as a man!" Bich says, her come-hither brown eyes twinkling. "For a female, you come work in Bui Vien Street as a girl, but you leave as a single mother!" She chortles, lifts her shot glass and sips her lady's drink. Tall but with a curvy figure that tempts men to fondle her everywhere, she has angular facial features and long hair frames her face, with disobedient curls at the sides. A floral spaghetti-strap top hugs her body and a mini skirt shows her killer butt and slender legs to advantage.

I lift my beer mug and empty it in one hard swallow. "Look at that beautiful sunset." I clink the frosted mug back on the metal table.

Bich and I are sitting on the sidewalk of Thien Dung Bar (not its real name) at Bui Vien Street, Saigon. Loud music is running riot inside the bar; thus, I chose to sit on the sidewalk with Bich so we can talk. A bright fiery orb is dipping below the seam of the cityscape, and rays of light are splashing a warm sensation on my face.

Bich tosses a gaze at the skyline and back to me. "I don't like sunsets." She crosses her long legs at the knees and tugs the hem of her red mini skirt down.

I fuse my gaze with hers. "Why?"

Her eyes dilate bigger as if revealing a secret. "A sunset reminds me of a painful experience."

"Can you tell me your life story?" I point at her shot glass. "Another lady's drink for you? I'll also give you a big tip afterward for sharing your story."

"Deal!" A grin plucks at her cherry-red lips and she spools me back in time ...

Five years ago ... Phu Chanh village, 20 miles northwest of Saigon
Birds flying home are silhouetted against the glow of the crimson sun as its rays melt on the fronds of the banana plants of a plantation. As Bich cycles on a dirt track to her home, she gazes at the sunset which soothes her mind. Outside the front porch of her wooden home, her father and the landlord of their house are sitting on a wooden bench. Bich brakes the bicycle, allowing it to roll on its own momentum to a stop.

"Bich!" *Cha* [Papa] jackknifes to his feet. "You're home at the right time." He casts his gaze at a fortyish man with a receding hairline sitting on the bench beside him. "Mr Ly is here to collect his rent – he's been waiting for a long time."

Bich gets off his bicycle and props it on its side stand. "But I gave you the rental money two weeks ago, didn't I?" Her gut cramps.

Twenty-two-year-old Bich works as a clerk in a small noodle factory, four kilometres from her home. Her mother died when she was seven and her father and elder brother grow bananas, sell the fruits in the market and also produce banana chips. She has two younger school-going sisters whom she supports.

Cha scratches the back of his head. "Well, it's like this, Bich." He clears his throat. "I went to Tran's coffee shop, had a couple of beers with friends and we played gin rummy and err ... luck was not with me – I lost everything."

"What!" Bich's jaw drops.

Ly rises from the bench. "Your father owes me two months' rent. They're past due. I want payment now! Or I'll come with the authorities to evict your family tomorrow!"

Bich tosses a shocked glance at *Cha*. "Two months rental?" Her heart thunders in her chest. "*Cha*, you gambled away two month's rental money?"

"Bich, please settle this problem." *Cha* turns and walks into the house. "I have work to do in the kitchen." He casts a backward glance at Bich. "I've a new order for thirty packets of banana chips."

Bich swallows the bitter taste in her mouth, throws a lingering stare at his father and then focuses her attention to the landlord. "Mr Ly, please wait here."

She takes a few steps forward, kicks off her canvas shoes at the threshold of the doorway and enters her house. From her dresser drawer in her room, she takes out some money notes and counts them.

In the front porch, Bich hands over the money to Mr Ly. "This is payment for one month. I'll pay you the balance end of the month."

Mr Ly waves his gnarled hand. "No! I'll not accept part payment." He releases an exhale of frustration. "I've been patient with your father's late payments for a long time. My patience has run out! And I haven't charged him interest."

"Please! Have pity on us!" Bich's eyes plead for sympathy. "We're poor!"

"Compulsive gamblers don't deserve any pity! I've bills to settle myself too!"

A weary sigh parts from Bich's lips. "Take this as payment

for one month's rental." She takes Mr Ly's hand and presses the money notes in it. "Come, follow me."

"Where are we going?"

"Just follow me if you want payment for the balance."

Bich walks from the house with Mr Ly in tow along the dirt track, lined with banana plants on both sides. After a hundred metres, she turns left and saunters to a spot further ahead where clumps of bushes grow. Scanning the environs, she tramps to the back of a bush, stands and turns to face Mr Ly, his face puzzled.

"I will give you payment here." Bich sucks an inhale to fortify herself and unbuttons her dress shirt to reveal full creamy breasts under a ratty bra. "You can fuck me as payment!" She unbuckles her pants, pulls down the zipper and steps out of them.

"Huh?" Mr Ly's grayish eyes bug in their sockets. "Wow!" He licks his lips. "This is a godsend!" He starts to unbutton his shirt. "I happily accept your payment!" Shadows dapple his pale scrawny chest as he hurls his shirt on top of a bush.

Bich spreads her clothes on the grassy ground behind the bushes and lies down, her heart stuttering in her chest, disgust thickening the walls of her throat.

Ten minutes pass.

"Aaarrrrgh!" Mr Ly rolls away from Bich and jumps to his feet, his testicles swinging from side to side.

"What's the matter?" Bich gets up to a sitting position.

"Tsssssk!" Mr Ly looks down, scratches his scrotum and pulls away a big red ant. "Ants have bitten my scrotum!" He squeezes the ant dead with his thumb and forefinger and flings it away. "Ouch!" He grabs another ant and kills it in the same manner.

Bich gets up, brushes her butt with both hands and starts to put on her clothes. "My debt is settled."

Saigon, 2017

Bich steps out of the shiny lift, walks down the corridor and spots the acrylic sign "Ban Flower Films" on one wall beside a frosted-glass door. She pushes the door inward, enters and finds herself facing a woman, probably early thirties, sitting at an acrylic curved reception desk.

"I'm looking for Mr Vo."

"Is it regarding the walk-in interview for an actress?"

"Yes, it is."

After having resigned from the noodle factory in her village, Bich arrived in Saigon a week ago to seek a better job, rented a room in the suburb but hasn't been successful so far. Yesterday, she spotted a vacancy in a newspaper for an actress.

The receptionist picks up a telephone receiver and says, "Mr Vo, another interviewee is here." She replaces the receiver in the cradle and thrusts her chin in the direction of a wooden door. "You may enter."

Bich raps on the door and enters the office room. "Good morning, sir."

Sitting behind an expensive-looking desk, a beefy man with greased-back hair and thick lips – probably in his early forties – thrusts an open palm at the visitor chair in front of him. "I'm Mr Vo – please sit down." He pulls out a drawer, takes out a sheet of paper and slips it in front of Bich. "Please fill in this form."

When Bich has filled in the form, she slides it across the desk to him. Mr Vo looks down at the form and, moments later, clucks his tongue. "I see... no acting experience." He leans back in his swivel chair, places his elbows on the arm rests and steeples his hands. "Now, let me explain the actress' role in the movie. Strictly speaking, we're looking for a body model."

"Oh, what's that?"

"The film we'll be producing is a love drama. The story revolves around an over-sexed woman and the movie has several sex scenes. The famous Miss Ngoc Suong [name changed] – I'm sure you've heard of her – will be the star. Her acting skill is awesome but, unfortunately, she won't do any sex scenes."

"Are sex scenes allowed in movies?"

Mr Vo leans forward and rests his big hairy arms on the desk. "Let me update you on the latest developments in our film industry." He throws a cursory gaze at Bich's décolletage peeking out of her V-neckline. "Our new film rating system allows adult content in movies." He harrumphs. "We've more or less adopted Singapore's rating system. P is for general audiences, C13 for viewers aged 13 and up, C16 for viewers aged 16 and older and C18 for viewers aged 18 onward. Full frontal nudity and simulated sex scenes are allowed – briefly, of course – but they must be relevant to the storyline."

"I see." Bich shifts in her seat. "So, what's the storyline of this movie you're producing?"

"A young housewife's husband meets with an accident. He is paralyzed and becomes impotent but she can't control her sexual desire. So, she has one affair after another, even casual sex with the newspaper delivery man, the postman and the plumber." He blinks a few times. "Now, being a famous actress, Miss Ngoc Suong won't do those sex scenes. That's where the body model comes in, replace her during those hot scenes. The audience will see a nude body but won't know it's not her."

"Yes, I understand – the body model is like a stuntman."

"Smart girl."

"How much is the pay? And how many scenes?"

"Before we come to that, I want to be straight forward – when can you spend a night with me?"

"Huh?" Bich's jaw goes slack. "What do you mean?"

Mr Vo chortles, revealing teeth that look like they belong to a piranha. "Because you've no acting experience, you must be fucked in *real* life before you're fucked in *reel* life!" He brandishes a finger in Bich's face. "In that way, your acting will be better!" A lecherous grin twists his lips and his tone of voice turns serious. "Every girl who signs a contract with me gives me something in return."

"So, if you sign a contract with a man, he becomes your cocksucker?"

"Whoa!" Mr Vo mocks a shocked look, spanning his eyes wider. "I like a girl who's vulgar! She's usually hot in bed!" He grins to expose his piranha-like teeth again.

"Sex can pay a debt; sex can land you a movie contract. That's why I became a bargirl." Bich pushes her lips into a thin line. "Use sex to earn big money." She adjusts the spaghetti strap of her tight top.

I grab a fistful of salted nuts from a platter in front of me. "Any unforgettable customers you've met so far?" I pop them into my mouth and start to chew.

"Yes." Bich runs her hands through her long hair. "At that time, I was working as a hostess in a nightclub." She bunches it at the back of her head, releases it and hikes her chin. "Can I get one more lady's drink?"

"Sure!" I thrust an arm in the direction of a passing waitress and raise one finger.

A few years ago ...

Mummy Nhung hikes along the corridor from the back of Crazy Horse Nightclub (not its real name) to the front lounge with five hostesses following behind. Togged up in miniskirts, they patter in stilettos on the marble floor, their hips swaying from side to side. Mummy Nhung, togged up in a pantsuit, crosses the hall between low tables to stop at a booth with a man sitting alone. Sentimental music from speakers soothes the soul, setting the mood for an evening of romance.

"Good evening, sir." Mummy grins like an enchanted ape. "First time here?"

Located in District 1, Crazy Horse Nightclub comprises a lounge with a dance floor, a bar counter and a live band on the ground floor, an open karaoke hall on the first floor and private karaoke rooms on the second floor.

Togged up in a plaid shirt with sleeves rolled up, the Vietnamese man looks up from the menu he's holding in his hands. "Oh, *bonsoir*, Mummy." He puts the menu on his lap. "Yes, this is my first time here." Probably in his early thirties, he has a handsome-looking face but a weak chin and big ears.

"Let me introduce my hostesses to you." Mummy moves to the side of the coffee table, turns and directs an open palm at one girl clad in a black bustier top. "From left to right, Cathy – in black and red; next is Thu, only nineteen years old; Bich, the third girl, just started work two months ago; France, from Hanoi, loves dancing; and the last girl is Vinh."

The man scans the faces of the girls and the corners of his lips upturn in a half-smile. "Bich."

Long hair tied in a ponytail, Bich moves to sit on the settee beside the man and Mummy goes away with the other lassies.

Bich turns slightly to face the man who has straight hair parted on one side. "Thank you for choosing me."

"Hello, I'm Charlie, Charlie Chiem."

Charlie takes the menu from his lap, thrusts it sideways and points to three separate spots. Bich snaps her fingers at a waiter who comes to take their order. "I repeat, sir," he says, looking at his notebook. "Plum sour whisky, mussels with Parmesan cheese, garlic bread, lady's drink, salted nuts." He goes away.

Tossing the menu on the coffee table, Charlie slides closer to Bich, his knee touching hers. "Who's your hair stylist?"

"Huh?" Bich's strawberry-red lips part in surprise. "Why're you suddenly talking about hair?"

"The straight pony tail is a classic but because you've a long face, other hairstyles are preferable." Charlie lifts her chin with one gentle hand. "You may want to consider full-length side bangs." He makes up and down motions with both hands at both sides of her face. "The bangs will give volume to your face." He cocks his head. "An alternative is a puffed hairstyle." He hovers a claw-like hand over his own head. "Clip the puffed hair at the crown of the head, leave the rest free."

"Are you a hairdresser?"

"Yes," says Charlie, nodding. "I was trained in Paris." He lifts both hands in front of him. "I've insured my hands for five billion Dong!"

"Wow!" Admiration fills Bich's curly-lashed eyes. "Where's your salon?"

"I don't own a salon." Charlie rests a hand on Bich's lap. "I provide in-call services. In that way, I do away with overheads." He slides his hand up and down her lap. "My clients phone me and tell me what they want. Cut, dye, perm, bleach, straightening?

I'll go to their homes with my equipment and products."

"Business must be good. Otherwise, how can you afford to come to a nightclub?"

"Many of my clients are female socialites of the city."

Bick jerks upright as a waiter approaches the table. "Ah, our drinks are here." She flings a gaze at four musicians taking their positions on a stage. "Our band plays jive music and rock-and-roll. You enjoy dancing?"

"I like the horizontal tango!"

Bich releases a little-girl giggle. "I know what you mean."

A bow-tied waiter sets two glasses on the coffee table and strides away.

Charlie lifts his tumbler glass. "Why don't you let me be your hairdresser?" He takes a long sip through the straw and puts the glass down.

"I already have a hairstylist."

"Try me." Charlie raises his brows. "First haircut is free." He lifts Bich's lady's drink and brings it in the direction of her lips.

Lips upturned in a half-smile, Bich turns her face away. "Thanks." She takes the glass from Charlie's hand. "I'm renting a small room, not convenient." She takes a swallow, continues to hold the shot glass and rests it on her lap.

"Why not come to my condo? I'm a bachelor so I live alone." Charlie flicks a gaze at the band as it starts to play a song and then back to Bich. "In fact, I've a few regular clients who come to my place for their haircut."

The door of the condo unit swings open to reveal Charlie standing in the doorway, wearing a sunny smile and a pair of beige slim-fit pants paired with a chocolate-brown t-shirt. "Welcome!" He swings his gaze at her feet. "You can come in with your shoes." He points to a wooden shoe rack a few feet away from the doorway.

Bich steps inside, lifts one foot and removes one sling-back pump. She repeats the process, takes both shoes and deposits them on the rack. Charlie closes the door, places a hand on the small of her back to steer her towards a leather tub chair. He settles down on another tub chair beside her. "Can I get you a drink?"

"No thanks."

Her gaze sweeping the living room, Bich spots a framed photograph standing on the TV cupboard. It shows Charlie and a bulky woman with the Sydney Opera House in the background. "Who's that woman in that photo?"

"That's my mother Mandy."

"Your father?"

"Oh, he died when I was young." Charlie takes out a glossy magazine from the bottom shelf of the low table. "Look at these hairstyles in this magazine. They're the latest in Paris!" He flips to a certain page and hands the magazine to Bich. "Which one do you want?'

The taxi stops outside Blissful Chinese Restaurant and Bich hops out. She takes long strides on kitten-heel shoes to its doorway. *Bah! I'm late, no thanks to the diversion due to roadworks.* She steps inside the dining hall and asks a cheongsam-clad waitress, "Charlie Chiem has booked a room. Which one?"

"Phoenix Room." The waitress points to the end of the hall. "There."

It has been three months since Bich got to know Charlie, and they've become close friends after seeing each other regularly. A week ago, he invited her to his birthday dinner.

Bich slides open the door to the private dining room. Her eyes span wider in shock.

A sorority of women are standing around a big table and singing, "Happy birthday! Happy birthday to you! Happy birthday to Charlie! Happy birthday to you!"

Charlie, dressed in a white shirt and a bowtie, is looking down at a two-tiered cake with one flickering candle on top and his hand is holding a plastic knife.

Sheesh! All his friends are old women! I wonder if he's a gigolo. Maybe after cutting their hair in their homes, he fucks them! But, again, that's only possible if they live alone.

Charlie looks up. "Bich! You're very late!" He waves his hand. "Come, join in the fun." He drops his hand at his side, flaps it outwards, and a few women shuffle sideways to make space for Bich.

Bich moves to step at Charlie's side. "Bich, these are my regular hairdressing clients."

Relief floods through Bich who nods and smiles. *Maybe I'm jumping to the wrong conclusion.*

Mandy dips her gnarled hand into her handbag, takes out a key and opens the door. She pushes the door inward, steps inside and kicks off her wedges shoes. A tight georgette dress encases her stocky body and it ends at her knobby knees.

She crosses the living room to enter the kitchen where Charlie is sitting at the dining table and popping a piece of pizza in his mouth. "How was business?" she asks, going to the fridge to take out a can of bird's nest drink.

Charlie closes the lid of the pizza box and pushes it away. "Three out-calls today." He rises and moves away from the table.

"You want to freshen up?"

Mandy pops the tab of the can, takes a glug and releases an exhale. "Sure, I want to change into something more comfortable." She upends the can to finish the drink and tosses it into a waste bin in a corner. "You've booked a table at the restaurant?"

Charlie walks to the living room. "I've secured a table where you can see the moon in the champagne." He settles down on a tub chair, picks up his mobile phone from the coffee table and fiddles with it.

Mandy enters the bedroom and, three minutes later, emerges with an ostrich feather duster in one hand. A pair of black brassieres and lacy panties are hanging from the hook of the rattan cane. Eyes glinting with rage, she walks straight to Charlie. "What's this?" She makes a face. "Filthy stuff that I wouldn't want to touch!"

Charlie jerks his gaze away from his mobile phone to Mandy. "Oh? This is a feather duster."

Mandy crimps her thick eyebrows. "I mean, what's at the end of the feather duster?" Her voice is like the caw of a crow.

"Bra and panties." Charlie meets Mandy's gaze. "What's that to me, anyway?"

"A pair of size-M panties and a B-cup bra. They're not mine – I wear size XXL panties and D-cup bra." Her voice brims with scorn. "You brought a woman here when I was away?"

"A client, actually – she came for a haircut." Charlie's tone of voice drips with guilt. "Then she changed to meet her boyfriend in a dance club. Must have forgotten her undergarments."

Motorbike-taxi rider Thuan leans against a lamp post on the sidewalk and keeps his gaze glued to the entrance of Crazy

Horse Nightclub. Two days ago, he met a rich middle-aged businesswoman who has offices in Saigon, Hue, Danang and Hanoi. For an agreed fee, she assigned him to tail her "nephew"— as she put it—named Charlie, and sent a photo of the subject to him via Zalo. Thirty minutes pass. The subject comes out with a tall hostess and they walk to a parked car further down the road. Thuan dashes to his scooter parked nearby and fishes out his mobile phone from his shirt pocket. "Miss Mandy, Charlie just took a girl out from a nightclub. I'll call you again from their destination."

Charlie and Bich lean against the side railing of Anh Sao Bridge in Crescent Lake Park and look down. A curved structure, the bridge traverses a tranquil lake. From the underside of its deck along its entire span, a curtain of water is cascading down, lighted up by LED lights of kaleidoscopic colours. Charlie and Bich say nothing to each other but enjoy the romantic scene reminiscent of a rainbow.

After a few minutes, Charlie wraps an arm around Bich's waist and she turns to look at him. "I'm not a perfect man, Bich," says Charlie, "but I love you perfectly." He pecks her on one cheek. "Let's go for a bite in a Japanese restaurant." He starts to steer her toward Crescent Mall.

"Sure." Bich's voice is like the whisper of an angel.

A barrel-shaped woman crosses the width of the bridge from the other side and shouts, "Charlie! Charlie!" She stops a few feet away from the couple. "Who's this woman?" Uplight beams from the concrete floor of the bridge illuminate the woman's thick neck, her cherubic face and her navy-blue empire dress.

"Huh?" Charlie almost jumps. "Why, it's you Mandy!" He releases Bich's waist and lets his arm drop at his side. "What're you doing here?"

Bich recognizes the woman from the photograph in Charlie's apartment. "Oh? Hello! You must be Charlie's mother, Mandy."

"That's what he told you, huh?" Her tone of voice is pregnant with disgust. "I'm his sugar mummy! I own the condo he's staying in!" Eyes blazing with fury, she plants her hands on her hips. "Charlie, you son-of-a-bitch! I sponsored your hairdressing course in Paris! I'm also paying you an allowance! And you dare cheat on me? Pack up your things and leave tomorrow. A man like you is not worth keeping!" She diverts her attention to Bich. "Miss, this kind of man is not worth being your boyfriend, too. Forget him for your own good." She stalks away.

* * *

Hunched over a writing desk in his room in Thao Cao Hotel (not its real name) in Bui Vien Street, businessman Robert Loo (a pseudonym) takes off his spectacles, rubs his eyes and puts them back. As he continues to study the draft business agreement which he will sign with his Vietnamese joint-venture partner tomorrow, his mobile phone on the desk beeps with an incoming WeChat message.

He picks up his phone to read the message and his eyes bulge when he sees the profile photo of the sender. In the portrait photo, a long-haired girl – early twenties – is smiling from an oval-shaped face, revealing white even teeth. Her deep cleavage promises lots of pleasure. *In Bui Vien, you don't have to look for sex. Sex looks for you!* He reads the message mentally, *Hi there!*

I'm Kathy. I am a university student. You want me for tonight?

He exchanges a flurry of messages with Kathy:

How much?
USD300.
Too expensive.
This is a 12-hour service. I am only twenty-two years old.
Can you come down to USD200?
USD300. Not negotiable. What you pay is what you get.
What will I get?
Massage, DFK, BBBJ, CFJ and A-level

As Robert reads the latest message, heat scorches his cheeks and his loins pulsate with desire. *Hah! I did the right thing by choosing a girl-friendly hotel.* Smiling to himself, he replies: *Let us do a short video call. Prove to me you are the girl in the photo.*

In the living room of a fourth-floor apartment near Thao Cao Hotel, six women – a few pear-shaped, others as scrawny as fossilized corpses, all in their forties – are lounging on chairs and watching TV which is blaring Vietnamese pop music. An overhead ceiling fan is pirouetting like the blades of a helicopter. The papasan of the vice syndicate is looking down at his mobile phone in his hands. Seated beside him is a young woman in her twenties, whose photo appears in the message that was sent to Robert earlier. Her shapely legs are propped on top of the coffee table in front of her.

"Shit," curses the papasan under his breath. "This prospect is no fool." He taps "video call" on the chat window in his mobile phone and hands it to the sex kitten beside him. "Ai Thy, another troublesome customer."

Holding the phone in front of her, Ai Thy smiles and says, "Robert darling, I can see your handsome face. You can see me? Now, you're convinced I'm real?"

"Of course!"

"Name of your hotel?"

"Thao Cao Hotel. Room 425."

"What time do you want me to come?"

"Nine? We'll go for dinner, then some dancing in Bojangles Club, near my hotel."

"Sure. Bye-bye! See you." She hands the phone back to the papasan.

Robert looks at his reflection in the dresser mirror as he combs his hair. A thirty-something man with broad shoulders, a long face and hair like a mop top is staring at him. He splashes Calvin Klein cologne on both sides of his neck and admires himself, turning from side to side. The doorbell rings and the front of his pants bulges with an erection. He takes long strides to the door and swings it open.

A forty-something woman, her face resembling a warthog, her body as stocky as a gorilla's, barges in. Up next is a lanky woman, totally flat-chested, wearing her hair like a hurrah's nest and garbed in jeans ripped at the knees. Before Robert can react, a burly man with penitentiary haircut and a tattoo on his neck bolts in and slams the door shut behind him.

"Mister, which girl do you want?" The thug's voice sounds like the bellow of an ox.

"Huh?" Robert's dickie and scrotum shrivel. *Shit! This is a bloody scam!*

Meanwhile, back in the vice den …

The papasan looks at the three mobile phones on the coffee table. Ai Thy is still sitting beside him, sipping coffee, her eyes glued to the TV.

A WeChat message comes in on one phone and the papasan picks it up. He taps "video call" and passes the phone to Ai Thy. "Another smart aleck wants to verify – a French man, Pierre."

Ai Thy puts down her coffee mug and takes the phone. "Hello, Pierre, can you see me? See? My photo's real, isn't it?"

Four of the old hookers – the other two now in Robert's room – laugh uproariously at a comical scene on TV and the papasan holds a gnarled finger to his lips. "Shh …"

"Where's Kathy!" Robert throws his hands up in frustration. "I booked her, not these two hags, err, I mean women."

"Kathy's busy with another customer." The thug's lips curl in a smug smile. "Please choose your girl." He plants his hands on his hips.

"Please leave, I don't want them."

"Then you've to pay a cancellation fee. USD20 for each woman. They came in separate taxis from far away."

"What!" Eyes widened in shock, Robert waves one hand. "No way! I didn't book them. Why should I pay?" He points to the telephone on the writing desk. "You want me to call security?" His forced casual expression belies the anger seething in him.

The door opens and another thug, wearing tinted blond hair and an earring, steps in. "Mister, we'll be waiting for you in the lobby tomorrow if you don't pay now." He holds up a big, hairy fist.

Robert's knees flutter and he yanks out his wallet. "T-Take

the money and leave."

* * *

Tottering along Bui Vien Street at 11:40 pm, I pass bars, nightclubs and massage centres where burly bouncers and young naughty ladies in hot pants and miniskirts are stationed at their entrances. Along the sidewalk, intermittently, there are food carts, cigarette vendors and freelance hookers sitting atop their parked scooters.

Ten minutes ago, outside a massage centre, a sex kitten – early twenties in age and wearing a spaghetti-strap halter top – blocked my path and asked, "Massage, sir?" She thrust a glossy leaflet at me. "You can have happy ending!" I held up a restraining palm and shook my head. "No thanks, I just want to walk."

And fifteen minutes earlier, a scrawny street vendor – a harmless-looking salt-and-pepper-haired Pops – with a two-tiered wooden tray hanging by a cord from his neck accosted me. "Mister, you want SIM card?" he asked, his voice like an old rooster's. "What about cigarettes?"

When I waved my hand, he continued, "You want marijuana? Cocaine also I have."

My jaw dropped. I sidestepped him and continued my stroll.

Ahead of me, four or five hostesses are sitting at tables outside a bar. As I am approaching it, a long-haired lassie and her companion – a middle-aged foreigner – harpoon my attention because a two-foot-high hookah pipe is set on their table. The bargirl takes the mouthpiece of the hose and takes an inhale. Then she leans sideways to her companion and – great balls of fire! – kisses him to transfer the smoke to him! The foreigner's chest expands and, seconds later, he blows the smoke out which floats heavenward.

A short distance ahead, thumps from a bass drum and twangs from a guitar gush from the entrance of a club. Just inside the entrance, a bouncer is pointing his finger at a Westerner and shouting, "Get out! Don't come here again!" The middle-aged Westerner takes long strides out of the entrance, his eyes narrowed, his forehead etched in furrows. In the sidewalk, a crack in the pavement catches his heel and he stumbles, falling flat on his face. Two passers-by laugh and walk past him, and a few others throw lingering glances at him.

I take two strides to the stranger, shove my hands under his armpits and help him to a sitting position. "Are you okay?" I squat next to him.

Togged up in a t-shirt and khaki pants, the man has a square face, a broad jaw and freckle-covered cheeks. He feels his right cheek. "Tssssk ... It's bound to get swollen and bruised." He mauls a hand through his short brown hair.

We get to our feet and he stretches one arm to rest a hand on my shoulder. "Damn! I need to sit down for a while, slightly dizzy."

I point to a restaurant a few doors away with tables spilled on the sidewalk. "Come, let's grab a drink in there." I extend my hand. "I'm Jackson – the beer's on me."

The man pumps my hand. "Nice to meet you. My name's Ethan (name changed)."

Minutes later, sitting at a small wooden table, I pop my can of Dai Viet Black and take a glug. "What happened inside the club?" My eyes flare wider as a light caramel aroma feathers the back of my nostrils. "You couldn't pay the bill?"

Ethan shakes his head. "Nothing of that sort. I was walking

on air and fell down to earth with a thud." He tugs away the tab of his beer can and fills his stein with beer.

Thus begins Ethan's story ...

Forty-year-old New Zealander, Ethan – an expat English-language teacher – steps inside Madeleine Club and the mamasan sashays on black ballerina flats towards him from the back of the hall, weaving between circular bar tables.

"Ah ... good to see you again, Ethan." Mummy's cherry-red lips tilt upward in a welcome smile. "So, tonight which girl do you want to book? Or you want to see a lineup?"

Ethan locks gazes with Mummy. "Who else? Tuyet!" He crosses his arms at his chest.

"Tuyet again?" Mummy's perfectly drawn thin brows inch up.

"Her killer body is my religion! Fucking her is my lithurgy!" Ethan chortles, revealing two prominent pearl-white canines. "I'm in love with her!"

"Hallelujah!" Mummy nods and thrusts an open palm to the brown, battered sofa in the nearest booth. "Make yourself comfortable – she's engaged with a client at another table. I'll try to disengage her."

Tuyet clicks her fluted champagne glass with Ethan's. "Cheers!" she purrs, her brown eyes as inviting as melted chocolate.

"Cheers!" Ethan's voice brims with happiness.

They entwine their right arms and take a sip each from their respective glasses.

Tuyet disentangles her arm and puts her champagne glass on the coffee table. "Teacher darling," she asks, placing a hand on

Ethan's lap, "which new word will you teach me tonight?"

Ethan pulls a ball pen from his shirt pocket, unfolds the paper napkin on the table and writes P N E I S. "Can you re-arrange this word so it becomes the anatomy of the human body?"

Tuyet leans forward to read the words, the plunging neckline of her top exposing a deep cleavage. "Anatomy? What's that?"

"A certain part of the human body." A grin sprouts on Ethan's thin lips. "It's most useful when erect." Eyes twinkling like those of a naughty boy's, he reaches out to pat her cheek with a gnarled hand. "I'll give you a tip of three hundred thousand Dong if you get it right. If you're wrong, you give me fifty discount on barfine!"

"It's easy!" yells Tuyet. "Penis!"

"Wrong! It's s-p-i-n-e!" Ethan purses his lips. "So, do I get my discount?"

"Aw, darling, you know Mummy won't allow me to do that." She slaps him playfully on the chest. "But tonight, I'll give my ultimate best in performance!"

"Aaarrrrrgh," Tuyet gasps. "There's a dull pain in my chest." She pushes Ethan away who rolls over to her side, and the bed they're lying on stops rattling.

In a state of nature, Ethan sits up on the bed. "Could be heartburn." He looks down at her, her big breasts rising and falling along with the heaving of her chest. "Do you suffer from gastric?"

"No, it's not gastric." Tuyet squints her eyes. "My goodness, my vision's blurring. I also feel dizzy." She presses a thumb and forefinger to her temples. "Dammit! I shouldn't have taken the Ecstasy pill earlier."

"What! You took Ecstasy?" Ethan gets down from the bed.

"Come on, you've to get it out of your system." He pulls Tuyet by her wrists and she clambers down from the bed. "Do you want to go to a hospital?"

"No! No!"

Ethan drapes one of Tuyet's arms over his shoulder and wraps one hand around her waist. Together they shuffle towards the toilet bowl in the bathroom. Tuyet sinks to the floor on her butt and hangs her head over the toilet bowl. Ethan sticks his forefinger into her throat and tickles it. Tuyet retches and vomits copious amount of foul-smelling liquid and some bits of food. Ethan scrunches his nose.

When she has nothing more to throw up, she rinses her mouth at the sink, and Ethan helps her back to the bed. He puts on his clothes, takes out his mobile phone for his trouser side pocket and taps its screen. "Hmmm ... It says here the victim should take activated charcoal to neutralize the drug," he utters to Tuyet. "I know a twenty-four-hour doctor's clinic nearby." He holds Tuyet's hand. "I'll get the charcoal from there – tell the doctor that I'm having diarrhoea." He releases her hand. "Won't take long, traffic's light at this hour."

Tuyet opens her handbag, takes out a key and opens the wooden door of her apartment. She swings the door inward and tosses a gaze over her shoulder. "Ethan, thanks for sending me home." She steps inside the doorway. "Come in for a cup of coffee, will you?" She presses her back against the door.

Ethan slips off his leather brogues, enters the doorway and steps inside a living room. *Hmmm ... it's decently furnished.* Tuyet kicks off her stilettos and closes the door.

"Tuyet! Tuyet! *La ban phai khong*?" A voice which sounds

like an old bear's growl comes from a room adjacent to the living room.

Tuyet takes a few paces to toss her handbag on a settee. "Ethan, please excuse me for a while." She points to an armchair across the settee. "Please sit down." She takes long strides to the room where the door has been left open and enters.

Tuyet's voice and that of the man's conversing in Vietnamese language come from the room.

Curious, Ethan moves closer to the doorway of the room and looks inside. A silver-haired man is lying on a bed and Tuyet, sitting on a chair, is talking with him. A wheel-chair is stationed at the foot of the bed. Ethan steps away from the doorway and plonks down on an armchair.

Moments later, Tuyet appears from the room and asks Ethan, "You want Chestbrew or Trung Nguyen? With or without milk?"

"Chestbrew brand is fine with me." Ethan crosses his legs at the knees. "No milk, please." He leans back in the armchair and scans his surroundings.

Tuyet crosses the living room to enter the kitchen at the back. A minute later, she brings a mug of steaming coffee and puts it in front of Ethan with a clunk on the glass-topped table. "You don't have any class today?" she asks.

"Who's that in the room?"

Tuyet moves to sit on the settee opposite Ethan. "My husband – he's bed-ridden."

"What!" Ethan sparse eyebrows shoot up. "You never told me you're married!"

"Now I have." Her matter-of-fact tone of voice sends a jolt to the pit of Ethan's stomach. "Is that important?" She holds Ethan's gaze for a moment. "Now you're getting to know me better."

"Err, you're not kidding when you say he's your husband?" *Sweet suffering saints! He's probably in his seventies!* "I mean he's old enough to be your grandfather."

"What do you mean?" Brows crimped in apparent annoyance, Tuyet reaches for her handbag, puts it on her lap and opens it. "That I'm lying?" She fishes out her mobile phone from her handbag. "Let me show you my parents." She runs a finger across the screen of the phone, scoots forward and thrusts it in Ethan's face. "See? This is a photo of me and my parents." She pauses. "The girl on my right is my older sister, now working in Vung Tau."

Ethan cranes his neck to look at the image on the Tuyet's phone. "But, err … how did you get to know him? Your husband, I mean."

"Five or six years ago, my father took a loan from him to start a business." Tuyet retracts her arm. "He offered me as collateral for the loan." She switches off the phone. "My father's business failed, and I had no choice but to marry him." She returns the phone to her handbag. "Two years ago, my husband suffered a stroke."

Ethan lifts his mug. "Any kids?" He takes a slurp and puts the mug down.

"No, he was impotent when I married him." Tuyet looks away from Ethan and releases an exhale. "Actually, I'm hoping he dies soon so I can inherit this apartment and whatever else he has and re-marry. You know, leave the nightclub industry and start a family."

"I see." *Aha! This is a golden opportunity to marry a soon-to-be widow half my age!* "Tuyet, I'd like you to know me better, too. So, I'd like to invite you to dinner in my studio apartment." Ethan's eyes soften, his gaze as gentle as a caress. "I live alone as I'm a widower. Just tell me what you want to eat and I'll cook."

"Oh, darling, I'd love to have dinner at your place." A smile pulls at Tuyet's lips.

Three months later ...

Tuyet flicks her gaze away from the glittery cityscape lights and orange-hued roads below to Ethan, sitting across her. "Darling, I've something to ask you."

"Yes, dear?" Ethan reaches out to hold Tuyet's hand resting on the table between them and leans forward to take a sip of his cocktail from a straw.

Tuyet and Ethan are in Eon Heli Bar on the 52th floor of Bitexco Financial Tower. Fifteen minutes ago, they were in the Saigon Skydeck on the 49th floor, admiring the panoramic views of the city.

Tuyet pulls her hand away from Ethan's grasp. "There's a business for sale." She unclasps her handbag with both hands and takes out a folded piece of news clipping. "Please read this advertisement." She hands over the piece of paper to Ethan.

Ethan holds the paper in one hand and reads it, "Restaurant in district three for takeover. Lock, stock and barrel. Owner retiring."

Tuyet cocks her head. "I've called up to enquire the asking price. I've only enough money for one third of the price. Can you give me a loan of one hundred and sixty million Dong? I can get a bank loan for the balance." Her brown eyes twinkle with anticipation. "This is an opportunity for me to start a new life."

"Tuyet, we've been seeing each other for several months –

and I love you." Ethan takes in a deep swallow of air. "Will you marry me when your husband dies?"

"Of course, darling." Tuyet holds Ethan's hands, interlocking her fingers with his and her lips curve into a beautiful smile. "Later, I'll bring you to meet my parents in my home village."

Ethan jabs the doorbell of Tuyet's apartment. *Bah! After giving her a cheque for the restaurant, she disappeared from Madeleine Club without telling me. At least, I know where she stays.* Several seconds pass. Ethan jabs the doorbell again and taps one foot impatiently.

The wooden door opens inward to reveal a man, probably early thirties, in the doorway. "Yes? What do you want?" His cheeks are sharp and angled, and his jeans ride low on his hips, unbuttoned to reveal a muscular belly.

"I'm looking for Tuyet."

"She's gone back to her home village."

"Who are you?"

"I'm her husband."

"What!" Ethan's jaw drops. "I've come here many times but I've never seen you before." His voice sounds strangled.

"I was working in Singapore."

"Jesus Christ!" Emotion jerks in Ethan's throat. "Then, who's the bed-ridden old man?"

"That's my father."

"He's Tuyet's father-in-law?"

"Are you stupid?" The man raises his voice a decibel. "Of course, my father's Tuyet's father-in-law!" Eyes shooting a hostile glare, he takes an inhale and releases it. "Now, what do you want?"

"I gave Tuyet a loan, and she has resigned from the nightclub."

"So? That has nothing to do with me!" He slams the door in Ethan's face.

Back to the present ...

"I continued to go to Madeleine Club and deliberately got friendly with another hostess." Ethan bites his lower lip. "I promised her a big tip if she could find out the whereabouts of Tuyet. A few weeks later, she told me that Tuyet's now working in Foxy Lady." The muscle in his cheek quivers. "That's where I was thrown out just now. When I confronted her, she uttered something in Vietnamese language to the bouncers and they forced me to leave." He mauls his face with one hand and shakes his head. "Never get involved with a bargirl – it's like playing with fire."

* * *

Inside a karaoke room in Silk Panty KTV (name changed) in Saigon's Chinatown in District 5, middle-aged Kim-Seng (a pseudonym) of Kuala Lumpur and his hostess Ava, twenty-something in age, have finished belting out a Mandarin song in duet.

Kim-Seng tosses the mike on the empty seat beside him. "Ask for my bill, please."

"Leaving soon?" Ava leans forward and presses the wireless service ball on the coffee table. "Come on, barfine me out." She shoots a coquettish gaze at his small and lustreless eyes.

Kim-Seng runs a hand through his tousled of tumbleweed-like black hair. "I can't – I boom-boomed too many times this afternoon." He lifts his mug of beer, upends it and slams it down on the coffee table.

"Mummy sells Viagra and Kamagra, a cheaper version of Viagra." Ava gives Kim-Seng a sideways glance. "You want? I can call her."

"Sheesh! It's dangerous to overdose!" Kim-Seng jerks upright. "I just two consumed two tablets today."

"Hmmm, then there're other alternatives. They're perfectly safe to consume in huge amounts."

"What's that?"

"*Hot vit lon*! It's duck embryo. Quack! Quack!" Ava chortles. "It's an aphrodisiac and also considered a delicacy! Of course, there's also the famous snake wine." She runs a hand down the length of his thigh. "Come, book me out for twelve hours and I'll give four additional hours free!" Her hand stops at his groin and squeezes it. "I can take you sightseeing."

Holding Kim-Seng by the hand, Ava steps inside a liquor store and walks straight to the counter, her heels clicking on the marble floor.

"Yes?" asks a young salesgirl. "Can I help you, Miss?"

"A bottle of snake wine for my boyfriend, please." Ava releases Kim-Seng's hand. "Sit down, darling."

The salesgirl studies Kim-Seng for a moment. "Oh ... at his age, he needs a combo." She turns to a cupboard behind her and opens a glass door. "We've three brands." She whisks out a bottle. "This brand is the best quality." She gently places the bottle on the glass counter.

Kim-Seng gasps in horror. "Holy smoke! Looks disgusting!" Inside the bottle is a cobra with a scorpion in its mouth. He scrunches his face. "Miss, you sure it's safe?"

"Of course!" The salesgirl's red lips upturn in a knowing grin. "The more poisonous the wine, the more potent it is."

"Get a big bottle, darling!" Ava nudges Kim-Seng with an elbow. "I can cowgirl you till I drop from exhaustion!"

The salesgirl lifts her dainty hand to her mouth to stifle a giggle.

Sitting on a plastic stool at a square table in an alley, Kim-Seng wipes sweat off his sloping forehead with a handkerchief and flaps his shirt-front to cool himself. Unbothered by the balmy air, Ava raises one hand to catch the attention of the hawker's assistant, a stocky woman in frumpy clothes.

When she comes over, Ava says, "*Hot vit lon*!" She raises four fingers. "*Bon! Kinh trong, Saxi.*"

A minute later, the same waitress returns with a metal battered tray in both hands. From the tray, she transfers four duck eggs set in small egg-cups, a bowl of *rau ram* leaves, a bowl of chili sauce, an empty plastic glass and a glass of Sarsi to the table.

Ava cracks the shell of a duck egg with a metal spoon and peels away the broken fragments until half the shell remains. Revealed is a small duckling's head and its curled body wrapped with yellowish yoke. She repeats the process with the other three eggs, spoons a dash of chili sauce to every embryo and pushes them to Kim-Seng. "Eat, darling!" A grin crinkles her face. "Pop a few coriander leaves into your mouth to mask the gamey taste."

Kim-Seng lifts up an egg and bites off a piece of the embryo. Wincing, he picks up a fistful of coriander leaves and tosses them into his mouth. He casts his gaze at the stars above as he chews. Ava opens her tote bag, takes out the bottle of snake-and-scorpion wine and unscrews the cap. "Sheesh! I forgot to ask for ice cubes." She snaps her fingers at the hawker's assistant and hollers, "*Nuoc da!*"

When the ice cubes arrive, Ava transfers them to the plastic glass with a pair of tongs. Then she pours snake-and-scorpion wine into it until it is full to the brim.

A full bladder wakes Kim-Seng. He opens his eyes and stretches his arms upward. Clad in a red lingerie dress, Ava is lying beside him, her eyes still closed, her hair cascading over her bare shoulders. They are lying on a mattress on the carpeted floor, which was transferred from the wooden bed. The previous night, the *hot vit lon* and whisky worked wonders and the continual impact on the mattress – akin to the force of a pile-driver machine – broke two wooden slats of the bed frame.

Kim-Seng manoeuvres to a sitting position, blinks a few times and gets to his feet. As he shuffles to the bathroom, he pulls his pyjama trousers down to his knees and kicks them off. He unbuttons his pyjama shirt, takes it off and tosses it on his former spot on the mattress. In the bathroom, he pees and takes a hot shower. While he is brushing his teeth at the sink, he looks at himself in the mirror. A chill shoots down his spine. *Huh? What's this red rash on my chest?* Kim-Seng barges out of the bathroom, moves to the mattress and gets down on one knee, "Ava!" He shakes Ava on the shoulder who opens her eyes. "You've given me venereal disease!" *Shit! I'm flying back tomorrow! How am I going to face my wife?* "Look at my body! Looks like an STD rash!"

Ava lifts herself up and peers at Kim-Seng's chest through sleepy eyes. "Calm down! I think it's just an allergy." She staggers to her feet. "I'll take you to a clinic. See what the doctor says."

I take a sip of my AK-47 cocktail and wipe my lips with my tongue. "So, was it an allergy?" I lean back in my chair, my eyes locking gazes with Ava's, sitting across a coffee table.

"Of course, it was!" Ava crosses her legs at the ankles. "An allergy is a small matter, just take an anti-histamine."

I scratch at my neck. "Hmm ...I'm feeling itchy." I lift a fork, stab at a fern-cake on a plate in front of me and start to eat it. "My God, what's wrong with me? I'm feeling itchy all over the body!" I put the fork down and scratch my back.

Ava's hand flies to her mouth. "Oh, my goodness, you must be allergic to the snake wine!"

"Snake wine? What do you mean?"

"When you went to the washroom, I poured some snake wine into your drink!" Ava bends down, exposing the shallow valley of her cleavage, and takes out a bottle from a shelf under the coffee table. "See?" she says, holding the bottle high in front of her.

Jesus Christ! It's half-filled with rust-coloured alcohol and contains a coiled cobra.

"Holy cow! You're trying to poison me?"

"No, darling, not poison you – I wanted to make you horny!" A little-girl giggle gushes from Ava's strawberry-red lips. "You know, make you barfine me out!"   She holds up one palm to pacify me. "Don't worry, there's a doctor's clinic nearby – I can take you there if you want to go."

***

"Hey, bartender," says Thomas Tsao (a pseudonym) stepping up to the bar, "give me Saigon's official cocktail!" He hefts himself on top of a stool and rests his hands on the bar counter.

In his thirties, he is donned in a form-fitting shirt and a little of his long hair has fallen on his forehead. He lifts both feet shod in Oxfords to snag them on the metal foot rests of the stool.

The middle-aged bartender, balding at the temples, scrunches his face. "Official cocktail?"

"Signature cocktail, to be more precise." Thomas' lips form a half-smile that seems to suggest that he is a man of experience. "You know, like Singapore's Singapore Sling, Manila's Manila Sunshine and Bangkok's Siam Mary."

"Oh? I see." The bartender blinks a few times. "I'll churn out a Mekong Cocktail for you."

Thomas forms an "O" with a thumb and forefinger. "Fantastic."

A tall girl sidles up to Thomas. "Hello, darling," she says, a sparkle twinkling in her big eyes. "I'm Charlotte." She reaches out an arm and slings it over Thomas' shoulder. "Where're you from?"

Thomas gives Charlotte a sideways glance and peels her arm off his shoulder. "Taiwan." He points to the adjacent bar stool with a palm. "Sit down, please."

Charlotte moves the bar stool closer to Thomas and plops her slender butt on it. "You want to boom-boom with me?" A smile twitches on her crimson lips.

Thomas swivels his stool to face Charlotte, his knees touching hers, his thick lips quirking at one corner. "Are you a ladyboy?" The tone of his voice is staid.

Charlotte releases a hollow laugh. "What makes you think I'm a ladyboy?"

"You're tall and big for a girl." Thomas snaps his gaze to the bartender as the latter puts a highball glass in front of him.

"Thanks." He returns his attention to Charlotte.

"My grandfather was an American G.I. That's why I'm bigger than the average Vietnamese girl." Charlotte slips the strap of her handbag off her shoulder. "Come, I'll take you to seventh heaven with my pornstar performance." She places her handbag across her lap.

"Can I see your ID?" Thomas sips at his drink. "Let me make sure you're a girl first."

Charlotte opens her handbag. "Sure, no problem." She takes out her ID and hands it over to Thomas.

Thomas studies Charlotte's face for a moment and eyeballs the photo in the ID, held in his hand. "Hmmm ... that's you in the photo." He crimps his sparse eyebrows. "Your real name's Trung Phuong Thuy (a pseudonym), date of birth is in numerals but the rest of the details are in Vietnamese language."

"See those words?" Charlotte points at a spot on her ID with her forefinger, its nail varnished shiny red. "*Gioi tinh* means 'gender' and *nu* means 'female'." She lifts her chin, flicks her gaze up from behind curly lashes. "You've a smartphone? You can check on Google translate."

Thomas takes out his moby from his back trouser pocket and taps its screen several times. "I see ... yes, you're right." He returns the ID back to her. "So, now, the magic question is how much?"

Charlotte slips her ID back in her handbag. "Short time or overnight?"

"I stay upstairs, so overnight." Thomas returns his moby back into his trouser pocket.

"USD three hundred." Charlotte checks her wristwatch. "From now until eight the next morning."

"Sheesh! That's expensive! Make it two hundred and fifty."

"Deal closed!"

Thomas braces his hands on the bar counter. "Bartender, a Mekong Cocktail, please."

"Oh, it's you again, sir! Sure." The bartender clears his throat loudly, then swallows the wad of phlegm he brings up. "How was Charlotte last night?" He bends under the bar and takes out a shaker.

Thomas scratches the back of his head. "Huh? You know her?" He leans forward.

The bartender grabs a bottle and pours in a dash of orange juice. "She freelances here regularly." He replaces the bottle nearby.

"Her blowjob was fantastic!"

"Yup, ladyboys are good at that." The bartender throws in something else in the shaker.

"What do you mean ladyboy? I checked her ID. She's a girl."

"Huh? Don't you know the law here?" The bartender pulls out a drawer and takes out a slice of lime. "Effective 2017, our law allows transgender people to change their IDs after sex-change surgery." He squeezes its juice in the shaker. "That means their new gender is shown on their new IDs." He tosses the squashed lime into a bin behind the bar. "Charlotte has been freelancing here for the past three or four years as a ladyboy." He pours the cocktail into a highball glass. "Then, she went for surgery and got a new ID." He plunks the highball glass in front of Thomas.

"Sweet thunderation!" Thomas' eyes widen in shock. "Yuks! I Frenched-kissed her!" He makes a face as if tasting something bitter and sticks out his tongue. "Pooey!"

Saigon Mamasans

Twenty-two years ago ... Yen Chi village

Quy – a twenty-eight-year-old widow – is rinsing vegetables under a sink in the kitchen when the telephone rings in her small living room. She turns off the tap, wipes her hands on her apron and strides on bare feet to the living room, its grey cement floor pitted and dull.

She lifts the receiver off the telephone cradle which is resting on a bureau. "Hello?" She tosses her gaze out a nearby window.

"Hello, convenient to talk?" asks Gia, his voice like a bull's bellow.

Heat waves from the tarred road outside make Quy squint. "Sure, my son's playing badminton, not back yet." She sails her gaze away, back to the coffee table in the living room.

"Can you get ready in thirty minutes' time? I've a client from Saigon but he's on a tight schedule. He wants a girl to be sent to his motel in an hour's time."

"Alright, I can make it."

Thirty minutes later, a roly-poly riding a scooter stops outside Quy's single-storey house. He parks the scooter under the front porch and ambles in.

Across the road opposite Quy's house, a wizened man in his living room pushes the split curtain of his window a few inches apart when he hears the chugging of a scooter. He peeks out. *Sheesh! It's that same man again. He comes to pick her five, six times a month.* A minute later, the fatso and Quy emerges from the latter's house. Quy is wearing a knee-length flared skirt and a tight top. They climb aboard the scooter which sputters away. *That woman's a disgrace to this village.* The wizened man shuffles to a telephone on a cupboard and dials a number.

Dong! Dong! Dong! A pimply faced boy is beating a gong, walking amongst an entourage of some twenty people parading along the main drag of Yen Chi village (name changed). Beads of sweat glisten on his forehead scorching under the afternoon sun as he continues beating the gong. *Dong! Dong! Dong!*

Another teenage boy walking abreast him holds a megaphone to his mouth and shouts at the top of his voice, "Prostitute! Prostitute! We caught a prostitute! We caught a prostitute and her client!"

A lanky silver-haired man who is the Head of the Commune is leading the entourage. Quy, her head lowered, and a forty-something beefy man – their hands tied behind their backs – are walking behind the headman. Behind the duo are four members of the Village Security Committee, continually shoving them forward. Earlier, they caught Quy and her john at a motel but Gia, the pimp, managed to bolt and escape on his scooter.

Several people come out of their homes to watch the parade and a plump middle-aged woman with a mouth and chin shaped for gossiping brandishes her pudgy forefinger at Quy. "Shame! Shame! Immoral woman! Shame!" She points at Quy's john. "Whore-monger! Shame! Shame! Shame!"

Back to the present ...

"I was put through a shame parade when I was caught with a

client." Mummy Quy's lips settle into a grim line, causing her chin to form deep wrinkles. "That was the most embarrassing moment in my life." She squares her shoulders and lifts her fluted glass. "Then I was sent to a re-education camp." She sips her cocktail and puts the fluted glass gently on the table. "Thankfully, shame parades have now been banned."

Sitting with my back rigid across a table, I stir the ice cubes in my watermelon vodka cocktail with a red swizzle stick. "How was life in the re-education camp?"

"Wake up early, exercise in the yard, eat three simple meals a day, listen to lectures and then do constructive work, such as making soft toys and woman's sanitary pads." A scowl creases Mummy Quy's mid-fifties face. "It was a tough and tedious period."

I feel discomfort in my bladder. "Excuse me, I need to go to the washroom." I rise from my stool. "Please feel free to order another drink."

In the washroom, I am releasing a stream at a urinal when a woman's voice behind me hollers, "Sorry, gentlemen, it's cleaning time!" I hear the slosh of a mop head being dunked repeatedly in a bucket of water. I turn at the waist to look at the woman. My eyes jolt wider in shock. Sweet suffering saints! Wearing a black patch over one eye, the charlady has a deformed left arm. She is now cleaning the floor by holding the mop handle with only one hand, its end gripped under her armpit.

Back at my table, I ask Mummy Quy, "I bumped into your charlady just now. Why did you employ her?"

"Charlady? What's that?"

"Cleaning lady."

"Oh? Her mother was an extraordinary woman."

"Really?" I pull my stool closer to the table. "Tell me her mother's story, please."

As Mummy Quy plays raconteur, mental images form in my mind ...

Binh Long village, 1965

Carrying a metal pail with a scoop inside, Dac-Khien goes to a wood-fired steamer which resembles a metal cupboard with several shallow drawers fitted with handles. He pulls out a drawer and steam escapes which floats away. Spread on the grille bottom of the trough are hundreds of skin-on cashew nuts. Dac-Khien scoops the cashew nuts into his pail and closes the drawer. He empties the other drawers, filling his pail with cashew nuts until it's full.

Then he goes to the next room where five girls – all in their late teens – are seated at a long scuffed wooden table. They are peeling off the skins of the cashew nuts with small knives. He distributes the cashew nuts to the girls one by one by pouring the fruits into their respective plastic basins.

Coming abreast to the last girl at the end of the table, he half-whispers, "Phuong, I'm resigning from this job." He pours the balance of the cashew nuts in his pail into her basin.

"Huh?" Phuong's sloe eyes look up from the cashew nut held in her hands and she turns her oval-shaped face towards Dac-Khien. "Why?"

"I'm going to Hue. Seafood-processing factories there pay higher salaries." He flicks a gaze at a partitioned cubicle at the far end of the hall. "I want to save for our future wedding. My friend in Hue says his boss has a few vacancies and –"

A stocky man inside a cubicle room at the far end steps to the wooden-framed glass door, opening it halfway. "Hey!" He stands in the gap with one hand on the knob of the door. "Dac-Khien and Phuong! Stop chatting! Busy yourself with work!"

Dac-Khien tosses a gaze at the owner of the cashew-nut factory and back to Phuong. "We'll talk during our lunch break." Dac-Khien strides away with the empty pail swinging from one hand and enters the roasting room.

Phuong leans forward and waves away a fly hovering above the dishes on the dining table. Seated with her around the table are her parents and younger brother.

The aroma of grilled meat and the scent of spices mingle with the cool evening breezes fluttering in through the windows.

Cha spears a piece of lemongrass chicken from a platter. "Phuong," he says, bringing the chicken to his plate, "it's time for you to settle down." He shovels a spoonful of white rice to his mouth and starts to munch.

"Huh?" Phuong flicks her gaze to *Cha*. "What do you mean, *Cha*?" She scoops some *canh chua* [sour soup] and slurps it off her spoon.

"I've arranged for you to be married to my best-friend's son."

"What!" Shock glazes Phuong's eyes. "But I've a boyfriend."

"That cashew-nut factory worker?" *Cha* laughs, exposing nicotine-stained teeth. "What can he give you? I heard his father is only a scissor-sharpener!" He puts down his fork and spoon. "My best friend owns a rubber plantation. He lives in Bao Loc village a few miles south." His gaze flits round the faces of his family members. "I've seen his only son several times. His name's Huynh, ten years older than you, decent-looking."

"My goodness!" Phuong's hand flies to her mouth. "So much

older than me?"

Phuong's younger brother jerks upright, looks at *Cha* from the corner of his eyes but says nothing.

"Phuong, your *Cha* wants the best for you." *Ma* says. "If we don't mind the age difference, why should you?" She lifts her glass of *nuoc sam* [herbal tea], takes a gulp and puts it down. "In fact, an older man is more emotionally stable than a young one."

Bao Loc village, 1966

A stocky rubber tapper, forty something in age, lifts her bucket filled with latex on the metal platform of a mechanical weighing scale in a field station, a rusty zinc roofed structure supported by four wooden posts. Standing behind her, five other female rubber tappers are waiting for their turns. All rubber tappers are paid by the piece rate; thus, their daily latex production are weighed for calculation of their monthly wages.

Phuong's mother-in-law slides a weight along the horizontal calibrated beam of the weighing scale until its end balances in mid-air within a small square chrome frame. "Six pounds!"

Holding a notepad in her hand, Phuong jots down the reading. "Toc Thy, six pounds." Two months pregnant, she is garbed in a loose tunic and a pair of dark slacks.

Toc Thy collects her bucket, shuffles on sandals to pour her latex into a big metal container nearby. A male worker stationed at the container uses a plastic bailer scoop to transfer the latex to a separate filtering machine to begin the initial stage of processing. When all the production of the rubber tappers has been recorded, Phuong and her mother-in-law leave the field station to return home.

Partway, Phuong's *me-chong* [mother-in-law] stops in her

tracks. "What's that sound?" She squints her eyes, peering upward through gaps in the overhead foliage of leaves. "My eyesight's bad – can you see anything?" The droning in the sky becomes louder.

"*Me-chong*!" Phuong points to her left. "Airplanes! Four big ones!"

"Enemy planes or American planes?"

"Probably American bombers, the enemy don't have such big planes."

The airplanes pass the vicinity and the droning fades away.

"What's this?" *Me-chong* holds an open palm in front of her. "Water droplets?" She brings her palm to her nose. "It has a bad smell." She rubs her palm against her pants. "We better go home fast and wash it off."

"My goodness! Several drops landed on my head!" Phuong starts to run.

"Don't run!" shrieks *Me-chong*, waving one hand. "It's dangerous for the baby! Just walk at a brisk pace."

Faces filled with anticipation, Huynh and his parents wait in the living room. Two hours ago, Phuong complained of stomach cramps and Huynh drove his jalopy to fetch a midwife. An hour passes and the cries of a baby is heard from Huynh's bedroom.

The midwife steps into the living room. "Sir, it's a girl. Both mother and baby are safe, but –"

Huynh jackknifes to his feet. "But what?" He shoots a glare at the midwife.

"You better look at the baby yourself."

Huynh enters the bedroom. His wife is lying on the bed, choked sobs wrenching from her lips, her eyes in a faraway stare.

He moves to the cot and looks at the naked baby. Shock blasts open his jaw. "Oh my God!" The baby has a deformed left arm and is blind in her right eye. Taking a few steps to the side of the bed, he points a finger at Phuong. "You've given me a deformed child! How am I going to face my friends?" His words are as hard and tight as the muscles twitching in his face. "Get out of this house tomorrow!" His voice is cold. "I'll send you the divorce papers later."

Saigon, 1968

Inside the dressing room of Tootsie Bar (not its real name) in Pasteur Street, Saigon, Phuong is powdering her face. She and four other bargirls are sitting at a long, cluttered counter stretching almost the length of the left-hand-side wall of the room. An equally long mirror is set on the wall above the counter and light bulbs on top of the former illuminate the faces of the lasses.

The door swings open a crack and Mummy Adele sticks her head in the dressing room. "Phuong, there's a man looking for you."

Phuong puts down her powder brush. "A regular customer?" She looks at Mummy's reflection in the mirror which shows a middle-aged woman with a bob hairstyle.

"I don't think so." Mummy Adele shakes her head. "I've never seen him before."

Phuong picks up a lipstick. "Alright, I'll be out in five minutes."

"He's sitting in the booth next to the jukebox." Mummy Adele closes the door with a soft thud.

Five minutes later, Phuong exits the dressing room, garbed in a halter top dress with low-cut back. In the hall, as the night is still young, only a few of a dozen tables are taken up by patrons. As she moves with a swaying bottom to the booth next to the jukebox, she gapes in shock when she sees the man lounging on the faux leather settee. "Huh! It's you!" She goes to sit beside him and holds his hands.

"Oh Phuong," says Dac-Khien as he binds his gaze with Phuong's, "why were my letters returned?"

"How did you find me?" Phuong's voice is as tender as the look in her eyes.

"Ah ... good to see both of you getting acquainted so quickly." Mummy Adele appears a few feet from the duo. "Sir, here's our menu." She thrusts a thick cardboard folder in Dac-Khien's hand. "It's Happy Hours, so there's a twenty percent discount on beer." She whips out a notebook. "One lady's drink to start off with."

"Tiger beer, big bottle." Dac-Khien tosses the menu on the coffee table.

Mummy Adele scribbles on her notepad and tramps away on ballerina flats.

"The culprit must have been my father!" Anger glints in Phuong's big brown eyes. "He must have returned your letters after he forced me into wedlock."

"I see." Dac-Khien crosses his legs at the knees. "Last week, I went to the cashew-nut factory and Thi-Hai told me you're working here."

Dac-Khien and Phuong are sitting on stools in the latter's bedroom in a fourth-floor apartment and looking out the window. Outside, the wind is howling. Raindrops are pattering on the pitted road and puddles are forming, illuminated by street lamps. Not a single star is in the sky and several lighted windows appear as squares of white in the buildings across.

Earlier at the bar, Phuong asked Dac-Khien to finish his drink quickly and leave but go to her apartment after the bar closes. She jotted down her address on a paper napkin and gave it to him.

Dac-Khien turns away from the scene below to face Phuong. "A year ago, I got acquainted with a few closet Communists who were my co-workers." He loops an arm around Phuong's shoulders. "They took me to attend underground meetings to learn about Communism. I'm convinced that Communism is the answer to our country's ills. Later, from Hue, I took a boat to Hanoi and joined the Communist Party." He pauses for emphasis. "Phuong, I'd like you to join me in fighting for our country's unification."

Phuong's eyes shine like pieces of jagged glass. *I hate Americans!* "Yes, I'm with you." A tiny wrinkle puckers at the edge of her brow in question. "But what role can I play?"

Off-duty Captain Perry Wilson (not his real name) – a thirty-year-old bachelor-hillbilly – of the US Marines lifts his mug of beer. "Cheers!" He takes a hefty swallow and hot blood pounds in his loins as he eyes Phuong's décolletage over the top of his mug.

Seated beside Perry, Phuong lifts her highball glass and turns at the waist to clink it against his frosted mug. "*Chuc mung!*" She takes a sip, licks her tongue on her upper lip. "Oh, darling, I wish you can stay here forever."

"I'll be back as soon as possible."

"Darling, promise me you'll always come back to me."

"I promise I'll never leave you."

From the jukebox, a melody begins and Karen Carpenter's voice starts to sing, "*Why do birds suddenly appear … every time you are near? Just like me, they long to be ...*"

"Oh, that's such a romantic song." Phuong puts her hand in Perry's and stands. "Let's dance."

They move to the dance floor and Perry puts an arm on her waist and one hand in her hand. Phuong rests one hand on his shoulder and leans on his chest, their bodies touching. They shuffle for a while and Phuong lifts her head and says, "Come to my room, darling. Let us smoke happy weed and de-stress." She coaxes him with fluttering eyelashes and a half-lidded smile.

"Great!" Perry's Adam's apple jerks in his throat. "I was a pot-smoking hippie before I joined the Marines!" His eyes shine with anticipation. "Gee ... Where did you get it?"

"The black market." Phuong winks. "Come, finish your beer and we can leave."

Phuong opens the door to her bedroom and enters with Perry following behind. She taps on a wall switch and a bulb illuminates to reveal a four-poster bed, a clothes closet, a dresser with a padded stool, two three-legged stools and a bureau cupboard.

She locks the door, turns to kiss him and leads him to the bed by the hand. "Please make yourself comfortable on my bed."

Perry plonks down on the edge of the bed and Phuong kneels on one knee and removes his shoes. "I'll prepare the happy-weed cigarette." She shoves the shoes under the bed and Perry puts a pillow against the headboard and leans back.

Phuong sits at the dresser, pulls out a drawer and takes out an old battered Jacob Cream Crackers box. She flips open the lid, takes out a piece of cigarette paper and spreads it flat. Then she takes out a pinch of greenish shreds and dribbles them along the length of the paper. *A bit of heroin will give this happy weed extra kick and loosen his tongue!* She adds a dash of heroin powder to the marijuana. Lifting the paper to her lips, she licks its edge and rolls it up. She prepares another cigarette for herself but it consists of a modicum of marijuana with tobacco.

Phuong replaces the Jacob Cream Crackers box back in the dresser drawer. "Your condiment's ready, darling." Rising from the dresser stool, she clamps the second cigarette between her teeth, takes the first heroin-spiked cigarette in one hand and sidles up to Perry, who's lying face up and whistling a tune. She puts the cigarette between his lips, snaps open a lighter held in her other hand and brings the flame to his cigarette.

Perry takes a deep inhale and holds the smoke in his lungs. Phuong lights her own cigarette, clambers on the bed and leans on the headboard beside Perry. Together they blow fragrant smoke upward which swirls around the room before escaping through the window. "I also have some whisky if you want it later," Phuong says, her voice like an angel's whisper.

They finish smoking their cigarettes in a few minutes.

"Tell me more about your work, darling." She holds Perry's hand and brings it to her big breast. "When is your next mission? I want to go to church to pray for your safety."

Perry squeezes her big breast. "I'll be leading a search-and-clear mission soon." His voice is hesitant and half-groggy.

"Oh, darling, you must be careful." She strokes his cheek with her fingertips. "Where? When?"

"Dong Ky village." Perry takes Phuong's hand from his cheek and kisses it. "About a week's time. Many of the villagers are law-abiding people by day, but by night, they're guerillas carrying out sneak attacks."

"You're going to burn the village down?"

"Nay, we'll flush out the Commies using a special thingamabob. It can detect hands that have held metal within the last twenty-four hours. They'll be arrested and interrogated."

"But those arrested could have held farming implements."

Glassy-eyed, Perry shrugs. "That's too bad for them." He turns sideways to peck Phung on the cheek. "I've my orders."

Inside a car parked on the road shoulder, special agent Khang (a pseudonym) of the intelligence division of the Army of the Republic of Vietnam focuses his pair of binoculars to look at the downstairs door of a shop house that leads up to Phuong's apartment. "This bargirl's always inviting officers to her place," he says to his partner Tai, a scrawny young man sitting beside him in the passenger seat.

"Perhaps she's a part-time hooker?" Tai takes a draw on his cigarette. "Many of these bargirls are." He turns sideways to exhale smoke out of the wound-down window.

"A hooker wouldn't be selective of her customers." Khang replaces his binoculars back in its case and leaves it on his lap. "This bargirl doesn't go out with rank-and-file soldiers."

The radio telephone on the centre console crackles and Khang lifts the receiver to his ear. "Yes?"

"Sir, we've triangulated the position of the transmitter," says a gruff voice. "It's in the building you're keeping surveillance on."

"Okay, we're moving in." Khang replaces the receiver and grabs a Halligan bar from the floor of the back seat. "Tai, it's action time!"

Khang and Tai leap out of the car and run to the ground-level door of Phuong's apartment. Using the Halligan bar, Khang prises the locked door off its hinges. They draw their pistols from their ankle holsters and pound up the staircase to Phuong's apartment. As fast as he can, Khang again breaks open the front door in the same manner. They dash in pistols first. The living room is dark and empty and they bolt to the bedroom, its door ajar and throwing out a column of light.

Wearing a pair of headphones, pyjama-clad Phuong is sitting at her dresser and taping the key of a Morse Code machine, which resembles a radio. She casts a side glance at the intruders and her face turns ashen but she continues to send her message.

"You're under arrest!" hollers Khang while Tai whips out a pair of handcuffs.

In the chilly dawn, six armed soldiers troop out of a prison building into the back courtyard surrounded by a high wall. Their boots crunch on gravel as they file into a single line to face a wooden stake sunk into the ground about twenty feet away. They stand at ease, their hands holding the barrels of their rifles which are resting vertically on the ground. Moments later, two soldiers lead a woman from the prison building to the stake and bind her hands behind her back.

"Madam Trang Phuong," says one soldier to the prisoner. "You've been found guilty of espionage and treason against your country by a military court of law." His tone of voice is emotionless. "You will be executed by a firing squad." He blinks a few times. "Do you have any last words?"

A choked sob wrenches from the dishevelled prisoner's lips. "Please tell my daughter Kim I love her very much."

The same soldier whips out a scarf from his cargo pants side pocket, blindfolds her and moves away. The other soldier goes to stand a few feet from the firing squad. "Ready!" Cracking noises echo in the courtyard as the firing squad cocks their rifles. "Aim!" He pauses for a tick and closes his eyes, as if unable to witness the painful scene. "Fire!"

Back to the present ...

"Phuong got exposed to Agent Orange dropped by American B52 bombers while she was pregnant with Kim." Mummy Quy clucks her tongue. "That's why she was born handicapped – real pitiful, was raised by her uncle. She drifted from one job to another until she eventually became our cleaning lady." A scowl invades Mummy Quy's face. "Phuong blamed the Americans for Kim's physical handicap and her subsequent divorce. That's why she hated the Americans, joined the Communist Party and became a spy."

Moisture sting my eyes. "Sigh ... what a sad story – for both Phuong and Kim." I pull out my wallet and extract a money note. "Here, Mummy, please give this tip to Kim." I pull out a second note. "And here's your tip." Mummy's face eases into a relaxed smile and I continue to hold my wallet in my hand. "Now, please get my bill." I shut my eyes and tears spill with reckless abandon.

***

Four years ago ...

A baseball cap jammed on his head, Cuong climbs over the low wall and steps into the window cleaning platform – consisting of three planks and measuring one by four metres – hanging over the flat roof of a four-storey office building. Tuan, mid-twenties in age, hands him two rectangular buckets, a squeegee and a scrubbing pad, both attached to telescopic handles. Cuong places his equipment on the platform and shows a thumb-up to his partner. "Alright, lower me down!"

Thirty-four-year-old Cuong and his partner Tuan operate a budget window-cleaning business using simple tools and equipment. A widower with two school-going sons, Cuong also supports his mother, who's in her early fifties. They stay in a small house in a slum in District 6.

Tuan steps to a make-shift gondola structure made of iron pipes and manually operates a giant pulley to lower the platform down, his forearm muscles bulging with the effort.

When the platform draws level with the sill of the glass window, Cuong places both hands to his mouth, looks up and hollers, "Stop! Stop! Stop!"

The platform becomes stationary. Inside the office room behind the window, a middle-aged man with a receding hairline is sitting at a huge desk and reading a document. He tosses a side glance at Cuong and looks down again.

Cuong dips a scrubbing pad into a bucket of cleaning solution and wipes grime off the window surface with vertical strokes. Then he uses a sponge-back squeegee to dry the surface. He looks up, sees Tuan and flaps his hand. Tuan lowers him to the third-floor window.

Cuong looks in the window through a gap between drapes half-drawn. A bob-haired woman, probably in her forties, is leaning against a swivel chair, her hands gripping the arm rests, her mouth gaping and closing as though in pleasure, her lower torso squirming.

Cuong's jaw drops! A pair of men's legs in dark pants with feet shod in loafers is protruding from beneath her wooden desk. *Jesus Christ! What're they doing?* He crouches, moves sideways and leans forward for a better view. "Aaaarrrrrgh!" Cuong loses his balance and falls down. The sidewalk awning cushions his fall before he lands on the pavement.

"*Cha*," says twelve-year-old Dat. "Can you give me some money? I need to buy new exercise books." He holds up a spoon and fork and casts a backward glance at the kitchen in anticipation of food.

Thirteen-year-old Dien looks up from the plate of rice in front of him. "I also need some money, *Cha*," I've been drinking tap water in the canteen for weeks, and sometimes I get a stomach upset."

Wheelchair-bound Cuong and two of his sons are sitting at a dining table in their house, waiting for veggies to be served. "Can you get it from your grandmother?" says Cuong, rubbing a weary hand over his face. "I've no more savings." A noisy exhale gushes from his lips. "I'm still looking for a job."

Moments later, his mother, salt-and-pepper haired Mai – in her early fifties – moves from the kitchen to the dining table with two plates of stir-fried vegetables and sets them down. "Come, let's eat, boys." She pulls out a wooden stool, settles down on it and picks up her fork and spoon.

Dat tosses a glance at Mai, a pair of spectacles perched on her nose, her hair tied in a bun. "*Bai ngoai* [Grandma], I need some money. *Cha* says he has no money to give me."

Lips gummed in a straight line, Cuong hangs his head down, his face a mass of agony.

"Dat, I'll give you the money afterward." Mai strokes the back of Dat's head. "I'm going to start looking for work tomorrow, a day job and a part-time night job." She places a hand on Cuong's shoulder. "Cuong, you look after the boys, okay?"

Togged up in a t-shirt and blue jeans, Mai dries the cooking pot with a terry cloth, places it on a rack and turns to look at the clock on the wall. It's 7 pm. Her shift as a kitchen helper in the restaurant is over. She goes to the punch-card machine at the cashier's counter where her employer is seated and clocks out. "Bye, Mr Ngo." Her boss grunts, "Hmmm."

Mai goes back to the kitchen, takes out her duffel bag from the locker and enters the washroom. She washes her face at a sink, enters a cubicle and undresses, tossing her jeans and t-shirt on top of the toilet cistern. From the duffel bag, she produces a black sheath dress and puts it on. She flips the lid of the toilet down, plunks her butt on it and removes her rubber sandals. From the duffle bag, she takes out a pair of kitten-heel pumps and slips them on. She collects her rubber sandals and clothes and puts them in the duffel bag.

Back at the sink, she applies make-up, removes her spectacles, unclips her hair and lets it down. *Yes, it works in the movies, and it works in real life. And the hair dye works wonders, too.* She struts out of the restaurant and hails a passing taxi. This has been her routine after having started work in the restaurant three months ago.

In the foyer of Nugget Casino (not its real name) in Nugget Grand Hotel on the bank of the Saigon River, Mai scans a group of four men walking out of the exit doorway. *They're too young.* She continues to wait. A couple saunters out with hands linked. Then, a silver-haired Westerner totters out with a walking cane in one hand. *Aha! A good prospect. Possibly staying here.* Mai approaches the old geezer. "Hello, darling," she says, fluttering her fake eyelashes. "Can I be your girlfriend tonight?"

The oldster stops walking, turns to face Mai and his lips part in a toothy grin. "Well ... well ... I'm delira and excira that I can still attract women at my age." His mischievous eyes twinkle with lust.

"There's a store selling snake wine down the road – if you need that stuff." Mai cocks her head sideways. "Come, I can take you there. Two shots will make you prance like a rooster crowing for its mate!"

"Nay, I don't need that, I brought my Viagra with me." He pats at his side pocket of his pants. "How much for long time?"

"Three million Dong. There's a love motel nearby. This hotel's strict, I can't go to your room."

"No problem with using a love motel." He extends his gnarled hand, and she pumps it. "I'm Bob from Dublin. Can we go for a drink in a bar first?"

"I don't mind some snacks." Mai starts to walk away with Bob in tow. "I'm Mai." She swings a side gaze at him. "Err, where's Dublin?"

The queen bed rocks like a child's hobby horse as Bob builds his desire to a climax with repeated thrusts. Beneath him, Mai groans in pleasure, her legs entwined around his waist.

"Ewwwww ... I'm coming ..." Bob gasps, shuddering his body. "Uuuuugh."

Earlier, in a bar, he consumed two Viagra pills with a bottle of Bia Ha Noi, while Mai snacked on bruschetta and French fries. Then they danced and chatted for a while.

Mai digs her fingers into his back as she soars to an erotic height and Bob collapses on her chest, panting and gasping for several seconds. They lay motionless for a while, and Mai taps him on one shoulder. "Come, darling, let's shower together."

Silence from Bob who is motionless.

Mai slaps him on the shoulder with one palm. "Bob? Bob?" With some effort, she pushes him away and he rolls to her side. "Bob?" His eyes are closed and he doesn't seem to be breathing as his chest isn't expanding and contracting. Mai manoeuvres to a sitting position and she scrutinizes his face. Heat creeps up her cheeks as alarm seeps in her, and she puts a finger under his nostrils. "Eeeeeek! He's dead!" She leaps down from the bed, her eyes widened in shock.

Sitting in the district police station, Mai dabs at her tears with a handkerchief. "So, that's the truth." She sniffs, her tone of voice water-logged. "I did not kill him."

The young police officer stationed at a big desk across her clicks his computer mouse and, seconds later, the printer at one side of the desk spits out a sheet of paper. He takes the paper and sets it in front of Mai. "Here, sign on the line below." He takes out a ball pen from his shirt pocket and hands it to her. "You'll also have to pay a fine of four hundred thousand Dong for being in a hotel room with a foreign man not your husband."

As Mai scribbles on the paper, a voice hollers from the doorway, "*Ma*! What happened? How did you end up here?"

The police officer tosses a gaze at a man sitting in a wheelchair being pushed by another younger man. "That must be your son." He returns his attention to Mai. "An autopsy has to be done. So, don't leave town for a few days just in case we've to ask you a few questions."

His shame is as thick as the shock in throat, Cuong fixes a blank gaze at the back of Tuan's head, sitting in front with the taxi driver. Beside him, Mai is looking out the side window of the taxi, her knotted hands resting on her lap, her lips gummed in a straight line. From the corner of his eye, Cuong flicks a fleeting gaze at his mother. *It's my fault! Ma prostituted herself because I can't work.* Guilt eats into his insides like acid and his breathing comes in halting breaths as he ponders whether he should allow her to continue moon-lighting as a hooker. *I'm useless! I'm useless! But what work can I do?* He feels as if he's sinking into a dark pit.

"We've arrived, Cuong," Tuan says.

Cuong snaps out from his thoughts. "Oh."

Tuan turns around. "I'll take your wheelchair out of the boot. Just remain seated."

Mai unlocks the front door of her home and enters the small living room. In the distance, a mongrel is baying at the moon. A month has passed since her brush with the law but nothing has been said between Cuong and Mai about the incident. She slips out of her kitten heels and sees a band of light from beneath the door of Cuong's room at the end of the living room. She taps on the switch of the fluorescent light in the living room. Then she goes to the kids' room, opens the door partway and pokes her head in. In the light thrown in from the living room, she sees her two grandsons sleeping on their separate beds.

Mai steps to her son's room and knocks. "Cuong?"

There is no reply. She knocks again. "Cuong, why're you still awake?" Still no reply. She fists the knob, turns it and opens the door. "Oh, my God!" Mai staggers backwards in shock, her eyes suddenly bursting with tears. "Oh, my God!"

Cuong is hanging from the bar of a window, his wheel chair lying on its side on the floor. A thick nylon cord is wrapped around his neck and its other tied is secured to the window bar. His fishlike eyes are rolled upward and his tongue is protruding from his mouth.

"After her son's death, Mai applied for a job here," says Bao, the balding bartender. "My boss took pity on her and gave her the post of mamasan." He puts a mug crowned with a frothy head on a paper coaster and slides it me. "She's been with us for more than two years."

I lift the mug to my lips, take a gulp and toss my gaze at Mummy Mai, chatting and laughing with a patron. As I observe this feisty woman, I recall what Henry James wrote: "Sorrow comes in great waves...but it rolls over us. And we know that if it is strong, we are stronger, in as much as it passes and we remain."

***

I pull out a notepad from my back trouser pocket and put it in front of me. "Which is the best seafood restaurant in Saigon?" I whip out my pen from my shirt pocket.

"I would say Tram Chin at Dien Bien Phui, District 3." Mummy Ngon brings the cigarette in her hand to her mouth. "Not only is the food fantastic, but the service is superb!" She takes an inhale. "The girls – all drop-dead gorgeous – will peel prawns for you, cut meat into bite-size pieces and transfer them to your plate, pour your drinks, crack crab's claws and pass serviettes to you." She exhales smoke through her nostrils which curl up like elephant's tusks before dissipating away. "They do all these while standing up – regulations do not allow them to sit with you. You're also not allowed to touch the girls." She taps ash from her cigarette on a Johnnie Walker ashtray in the centre of the table. "At the end of your meal, you pay a mandatory tip."

Face covered with age spots, Mummy Ngon, probably in her early seventies, and wearing short shiny black hair – obviously dyed – and I are chatting in an all-talk-no-action bar in Saigon's Chinatown. In such a bar, a hostess cannot be barfined out: they only talk to entertain clients.

"Wow!" I jot down the restaurant's address in my notebook. "Which are some of the more special KTV bars in Saigon?"

"Sunflower KTV and Sunlight KTV – both owned by the same management. Their hostesses wear transparent negligee and no bras during the lineup."

"Address, please – it's for the benefit of my readers."

"Sunflower is in Nguyen Trai Street, and Sunlight is in Ton That Tung Street. They're both in District 1." Mummy Ngon swings her gaze sideways, smiles at a patron passing our table and returns her attention to me. "Last year, police raided two restaurants at Ton That Tung Street which is a popular shopping spot. DMax Restaurant and Ruby Restaurant were hit. They were operating karaoke rooms without license and employed hostesses without any employment contracts."

I slip my pen behind one ear. "Apart from these two, any other special places?" I lift my stein and throw another swallow of beer down my throat.

"I also recommend New Stocking in Nam Ky Khoi Nghia Street. All their hostesses wear sexy stockings. You can tear away their stockings if you want to – that's a pretext for you to fondle their legs and thighs." She pauses as she pours more beer into my mug. "But an extra charge of ...err ... I think around three hundred thousand Dong is imposed."

"Sheesh!" I make a face. "So expensive for a cheap thrill? Any cheaper place?"

"You want something cheaper?" Thin wrinkled lips upturned in a smirk, Mummy Ngon hops down from her bar stool to the floor, her saggy breasts swinging from side to side in her loose top. With both hands, she hitches up her knee-length skirt to mid-thigh, revealing scrawny stockinged legs, and rests one foot shod in leather brogue on the footrest of her bar stool. "You can rip off my stockings for half that price!"

I gape and recoil in horror.

Café Girls, Hot Toc Girls and Gai Goi

I lift my cup of coffee and take a sip. "Can you show me a few interesting places not seen by normal tourists?" I jerk upright as a bitter tang of caramelisation balances out the sugar sweetness on my taste buds.

Am sucks at a straw and licks her red lips which are shaped like a Cupid's bow. "Since you're a writer, I can take you to Book Street, Flower Street and then go for lunch at a cannabis bar – that'll give you something to write about." Her dark brown hair – obviously tinted – frames a delicate oval face and a loose t-shirt hangs loosely on her slender frame.

Am and I are sitting in Sapphire Coffee (name changed), an all-talk-no-action café in District 1, and her life story is nothing to write home to my Mom about.

Saigon has three types of cafes; namely, regular cafes; all-talk-no-action cafes and hugging cafes (popularly known as *caphe om*). In an all-talk-no-action café, a girl comes to sit with you and talk – nothing more – in return for a tip. In a hugging café, the degree of physical contact varies with each establishment, and can range from smooching to sex.

"Huh?" My jaw goes slack. "Marijuana?"

Am nods.

I force my gaze away from her sexy lips. "Great balls of fire! Is it legit?"

Am shrugs. "I'll pick you up on my moped tomorrow." She

sucks at the straw again until it makes loud gurgling noises at the bottom of the glass. "Nine o'clock in the morning."

"Sure." I flip out a notebook and my ball pen. "Can you name a few famous *caphe om*? I want to give readers of my book their money's worth."

"At Pham The Hien Road in District 8, there're Café 714, Hai Yen Café, Phuc Nguyen Café and Diem Cong."

A waitress places an aluminum platter on my table. I toss payment on the platter and pass a tip to Am. "See you tomorrow," I say, rising to my feet.

I stand with my back facing Notre Dame Cathedral and Am snaps a photo of me with my handphone. She returns the handphone to me and we walk toward Nguyen Van Binh which links Cong Xa Paris Square to Hai Ba Trung Street.

Earlier, we strolled in Ho Thi Ky Flower Market at Le Hong Phong Street where the beauty of daisies, marigolds, roses, gerberas, orchids and other mind-boggling varieties of blooms suck my breath away. Am recommended that I try the fish noodle at the Cambodian market but I found it so-so only.

Book stores and cafes line both sides of the one-hundred-metre-long Nguyen Van Binh, with trees and potted plants creating a serene atmosphere. "Vietnam has an annual book fair," Am says, diving into a kiosk, "and Vietnam Book Day is celebrated to promote a reading culture."

I follow her and browse the titles. Most of the books are in Vietnamese language but English and French titles are also available. Other stores also carry old books, stationery, magazines and newspapers. We step into a café, order coffee and snacks and Am whips out her smartphone. She taps the screen a few times and shows it to me. "See? This is the Facebook of Dreamer Hood. I'll take you there after our coffee."

I take her phone, place it in front of me and scroll its Facebook pages. The postings of the café on its timeline show that the following are available: canna-infused croissant, pre-rolled joint, cannabis cheese cake, cannabis smoothie, cannabis-infused peanut butter, cannabis popcorn, canna burger and many more. Address: No. 18 Nguyễn Văn Thủ, Đa Kao Ward, District 1.

***

Eight years ago ...

Holding an oiled paper umbrella, Nhung plods on wobbly legs into the bus station of Bac Lieu town, 260 km south of Saigon. A cloth bag containing some clothes and a bottle of water hangs from her shoulder. She closes the umbrella and dangles it in one hand from the loop of cord at its handle. Stepping to the ticketing counter, she looks at a sign displaying bus fares and departure times. *Sheesh! I don't have enough money to buy a ticket to Saigon.* She spots three buses parked at one end of the building and saunters towards them. One of them has a two-feet-by-one-foot sign with the words "Bac Lieu-Saigon" propped against the inside of its windscreen. A beefy man is sitting in the driver's cabin – its window rolled down – and reading a newspaper.

Nhung moves to the driver's side. "Sir," she calls out, looking up, "I don't have enough money for a ticket. Can you let me sit on the floor?" She dips her hand in her side pocket of her pants pocket, grabs a few coins and shows them to the driver.

"No, I can't," says the driver, casting his gaze down at Nhung. "If a ticket inspector boards the bus, I'll be in trouble."

Three hours ago, nineteen-year-old Nhung left her home village and walked to Bac Lieu town, eight kilometres away. Two days ago, she quarrelled with her father and ran away from home. Nhung's mother died while giving birth to her and, because of this, her *Cha* has never treated her well.

"Please help me, sir. I need to go to Saigon desperately."

"I can put you in the luggage compartment if don't mind."

"Sure." Extending her arm, she hands the coins over to the driver who takes them.

Sitting cramped in the luggage compartment between two stacks of suitcases, Nhung blinks as sweat trickles down her face, stuffy air almost suffocating her. The roar of the bus engine which sounds like a giant waterfall tumbling down is causing her a headache. More than an hour passes. *My goodness! I feel like fainting!* Holding down a retch, Nhung repeatedly thumps the roof, just inches above her head, with a fist. Seconds later, she feels the bus coming to a stop and the compartment door is yanked open from the outside. Nhung squints at the bright lights and gets down, clutching her umbrella and cloth bag with both hands.

The bus driver hikes his chin, his eyes filled with ire. "What's the matter?"

Nhung takes in great gulps of air before she gasps, "It's too hot inside! Too noisy also!" She shrugs her shoulders to get the kinks out and sees that the bus has stopped under a big shady tree.

"Then I've no choice but to leave you here!" The bus driver closes the door of the luggage compartment. "You're nothing but trouble!" He strides to his cabin, climbs aboard and drives off, the bus spitting exhaust fumes in her face.

Oh shit! I'm stranded! Taking stock of the situation, Nhung steps to the road shoulder, waits and jerks a thumb as a car comes by. The car driver ignores her. Minutes pass. A truck rumbles down the road, and Nhung jerks her thumb in the direction it is going. The truck slows to a halt and Nhung gasps in horror. The bonnet of the truck is tied to its fender with wires and its wheels have rusted to the colour of copper.

A grey-haired geezer shifts sideways in his seat and asks, "You want a ride?" His voice sounds like a crow with a cold.

"Sure, I want to go to Saigon."

The geezer scratches at his stubbly chin. "How much can you pay?"

"Huh?" Nhung considers for a moment and takes off her small jade pendant hanging from her neck by a cord. "I've no money but you can have this jade pendant."

The geezer waves his gnarled palm. "Alright, get in."

One year later …
Nhung steps up to the closed wooden door of Lang Man Nightclub (not its real name) in District 1 and jabs a button at its side. A small window slides to one side to reveal a peep hole about five by two inches and a pair of eyes on the other side. "Yes?"

"I'm looking Mr Hien Lac. It's regarding the post of hostess as advertised in the newspaper."

"Alright, come in." The voice is squeaky.

The window slides back in place and there is the sound of a bolt grating in its catch and a rattle of a key in a lock. The hinges squeal as the door swings inward and Nhung enters a dim hall filled with low coffee tables and plush tub chairs. The forty-something man closes the door and locks it.

"Please follow me, Miss." The man starts to stride away.

Nhung follows him to a room at the back of the hall and the latter knocks on the door. He opens it a crack, sticks his head in and says, "Sir, an interviewee for the post of hostess."

"Send her in."

The man pushes the door fully open for Nhung to enter and then closes it.

Nhung finds herself in a big bright room with a lean early thirties man sitting behind a shellacked desk reflecting the overhead lights. Rolled-up sleeves of a crisp white shirt reveal muscular forearms covered with hair. His face is ruddy and is ravaged with old acne scars.

"Good afternoon, Mr Hien Lac."

Mr Hien Lac juts his jaw at the visitor's chair opposite him, pulls out a drawer and takes out a sheet of paper. "Please fill this up." He turns the paper top side up and slides it across the table to Nhung.

Nhung looks down at the paper, places her handbag on her lap and takes out a ball pen. While she is filling in the form, Mr Lac's small eyes rake her from her face to her ample chest and down to her slender arms and dainty hands.

When the form is completed, Nhung hands it over.

Mr Lac looks down at the form. "Hmm …you're now a supermarket cashier, previous job was sales assistant in a lingerie store. Now, this job as hostess involves entertaining men, making them happy. Basic salary plus commission on lady's drinks and barfines can be three, four or even five times your present salary." He leans back his chair, rests his elbows on its arms and steeples his hands. "Training will be provided – how to uncork a champagne bottle, pour beer without the froth over-spilling, light a cigarette, operate the karaoke system, sing songs and entertain men."

"I don't have much experience drinking hard liquor."

"Don't worry about that. Our lady's drink is very diluted, almost like plain water but very expensive." He jabs a finger in the direction of her chest. "That's one way we make money." Mr Lac leans forward and rests his arms on the desk. "When can you start work?"

"As soon as possible."

"How about tomorrow?"

"Good! You have any sexy clothes? Like miniskirts, spaghetti strap tops, tank tops, bare-back blouses? And also stilettos."

"Err, no."

"You need to wear those clothes to attract men."

"Can I buy them later – after I get my first month's salary?"

Mr Lac searches her face, his eyes weighing her words. "I see, you've no money." He ponders for a second. "I'll give an advance salary then. At the end of the month, I'll settle your commission." He shifts a hip, pulls out his wallet from his side pocket and slips out a stack of money notes. "Here you are." He leans forward and hands over them over.

"Thank you, sir."

Mr Lac pulls out a top right drawer, takes out a receipt pad and scribbles on the front page. "Please sign here." He takes back the pad and replaces it in the drawer. "So, I'll see you tomorrow at around this time. We'll start your training tomorrow." His thick lips curve into a satisfied smile. "Happy shopping."

The next day ...
Togged up in a pair of denim hot pants with ribbed holes and a dark cropped top, Nhung stands in front of Mr Lac's desk and turns a circle. "What do you think of this outfit, sir?"

Eyes bugging wide, Mr Lac nods as he stares at Nhung, his eyes drinking her in like a man in a drought. "Yes! Looks like you're cut out to be a successful nightclub hostess!"

"Thank you, sir."

Mr Lac rises. "Now, let's go to the training room." He rounds his desk and leaves the room with Nung in tow.

In the hall, they climb up a wrought iron circular staircase, walk down a corridor between rows of karaoke rooms. At the end of the corridor, Mr Lac stops at a door with the words "Training Room" on a bronze plate, fishes out a key from his trouser side pocket and opens it.

He steps inside, taps a light switch and wall lights bath the room in romantic saffron lights. Nhung enters the room and her eyes bulge in shock. At the left wall of the room is a four-poster queen bed and at the right is a velvet sofa paired with a coffee table.

Mr Lac locks the door and steps out of his loafers. "Come, I'll teach you the see-saw, the reverse doggy and the standing disco sex positions!" Small eyes glinting with lust, he starts to unbutton his shirt.

"What!" Nhung's mouth sags.

One month later ...

Sitting at his desk, Mr Lac looks down at a dog-eared ledger in front of him. "Nhung, you've failed to hit this month's quota." His eyes are as cold as ice. "What's the problem?" His voice is as hard as stone.

Sitting across Mr Lac, Nhung shifts in her seat. "Err, maybe I lack conversational skills." Her pulse quickens.

Mr Lac pulls out a bottom drawer and takes out a packet

of condoms. "You need more training!" He stands up and the leather cushion seat whooshes upward. "Come, let's go to the training room."

"Huh! Again?" Shards of ice prickle Nhung's spine.

Back to the present ...
"My former papasan was a lecherous bastard!" Nhung guzzles her lady's drink and puts the glass down. "He has fucked every hostess in his nightclub."

For a petite girl, she is shapely in the right places, perfectly symmetrical. Long shiny hair dances in loose wisps on her shoulder and neck. A beige long-sleeved loose-fitting top and belted khaki slacks give her a girl-next-door appearance.

I pick up a brownie. "How long were you there?" I pop it into my mouth.

Nhung and I are chatting in a hugging café. According to her mamasan, there are rooms upstairs for private moments with hostesses.

"I lasted only six months there." Nhung straightens up and adjusts the chrome buckle of her tortilla-coloured belt. "Then I joined a golf club as a caddy."

A golf course ...
Crowned with a cap, Yamamoto (not his real name) – an early-thirties tourist on a golfing vacation – squints at the sprawling expanse of Bermuda grass in the green. He wriggles his butt, looks down at the golf ball, waggles the club and swings it up above his shoulders. Then he swings the club down to hit the ball. *Thud!* The ball takes flight but goes askew. "Drat!" Yamamoto punches the air in frustration.

Standing a few feet away, Nhung cocks her hip sideways and pats it. "Sir, in the downswing, you must use your hips." She straightens her left arm. "Your lead arm – that's your left arm – should be straight." Togged up in a cap and a tight long-sleeved t-shirt straining at her ample bosom, Nhung steps to a buggy nearby, picks up another ball from a bucket and goes to place it on the plastic tee. "Come, try again." She steps away from the Yamamoto.

"Can you show me how?" Yamamoto twists sideways at the waist to face Nhung. "I mean, go through the motions with me?" He gets back to a tee-off stance.

Nhung steps behind Yamamoto, circles her arms around him and holds his hands gripping the club. "Relax your body, sir." She presses her breasts against Yamamoto's back and breathes down his neck. "Ready? One, two, three!" Together, they swing the club up and down. *Thud!* The ball zooms into the air. Nhung releases Yamamoto and places one hand over her eyes, her gaze following the ball. It flies straight but falls a short distance away from a yellow flag.

Yamamoto removes his cap and holds it in his hand. "What's wrong now?" He scratches the side of his head and replaces the cap.

"It's your grip, sir." Nhung forms a fist with her right hand. "Too tight, too stiff! A famous American golfing instructor once said that gripping a club is like holding a bird. Don't hold too tight as to crush it, but not too loose as to let it fly away."

"Can you show me?" Yamamoto's eyes glint with lusty intent.

Nhung steps behind Yamamoto, wraps her arms around his waist, pressing her breasts against his back. Looking around to make sure no other golfer is nearby, she slides one hand to his crotch, squeezes it and holds the grip. "This is the right amount of pressure! You feel it?"

Yamamoto's jaw drops. "Yes! Yes!" His eyes screw upward in pleasure. "The pressure's right! My bird's singing with joy!"

An hour later, Nhung steers the buggy onto the front porch of the clubhouse. "Here we are, sir." She casts a coquettish gaze at the Japanese golfer, fluttering her eyelashes. "Enjoy your dinner tonight, sir."

Yamamoto pulls out his wallet, slips out a US$50 bill and hands it to Nhung. "Your tip, Nhung."

"Thank you, sir." Nhung slips the money note into her side pants pocket.

Locking his gaze with Nhung's, Yamamoto now takes out a US$100 bill, tears it in half and passes one half to her. "The other half is yours if you come to my hotel room tonight. I'll text you my room number if you care to give me your handphone number."

Back to the present ...

I adjust my collar and rest my elbows on the table. "Why did you resign from the golf club?"

"I didn't resign." Nhung twirls a lock of hair around her right forefinger. "Gossip of my crotch-grabbing antics reached my employer's ears, and he sacked me." Her forefinger stills and the curl of hair springs free and spirals to her shoulder.

"How long where you there?" I flap a hand at a passing waitress and points at Nhung's near-empty glass. "One more lady's drink."

"Two years."

Mummy – officially known as the café supervisor – togged

up in a pantsuit, comes to our table. "Sir," she says, revealing a mouth full of uneven teeth, "you're sure you don't want to book Nhung upstairs?"

I smile at Mummy, shake my head and return my attention to Nhung. "Are you S, M or D?"

Nhung draws her eyebrows together in question. "What's that?"

"Single, married or divorced?"

"Divorced – I was married for two years."

I pick up another chocolate brownie. "Oh? What happened?" I dunk it into my coffee.

Four years earlier ...
Sitting in a cybercafe, Nhung logs onto Facebook Messenger. Among her Facebook friends is Du-Ho (name changed) of Seoul who is online.

> *Hi here, Nhung!*
> *Good evening, Du-Ho. Taken your dinner?*
> *Yup, what about you? Your shift over?*
> *Yes, I'm doing the morning shift this week.*
> *Tonight, my tae-kwando class was cancelled, that's why I'm able to go online to chat with you.*

Two months ago, Im Du-Ho, aged thirty, received a Friend Recommendation on Facebook for Nhung Mieu. He checked her profile and saw: Working as a barista in Nui Tuong Café, District 1, Saigon. When he clicked on the photo section which contained several images, his loins tingled at the sight of her cleavage in her plunging neckline and the suggestion of nubile curves beneath her dress. He clicked "Accept" which birthed a long-distance relationship. Handpicked to head his employer's branch office in Saigon which was scheduled to open in six months' time, Du-Ho has been actively seeking Vietnamese female friends over the past two months.

Two years later ...

Nhung spreads butter on a piece of toast, puts down the knife and takes a bite. Crumbs fall from the edge of the toast to the table and, with her palm, she sweeps them aside into a small pile.

Sitting across the dining table, Du-Ho flicks his gaze from the tabloid newspaper spread diagonally in front of him to his wife. "Darling, I've a dinner appointment with a client this evening. You've to eat alone, I'm afraid." He lifts the pot in the centre of the table, fills his own cup with coffee and holds the former in mid-air. "More coffee, darling?"

Nhung takes a swallow and nods. "Yes, please."

Du-Ho refills her cup and replaces the pot back in its former spot.

Nhung lifts her cup, takes a sip and puts it down. "Ugh!" She holds back a retch, one hand flying to her mouth. "My God, I feel sick!" She makes a face. "I've been like his for almost a week; I'm also having body aches."

"Huh? Must be morning sickness!" Du-Ho shoots to his feet, causing the legs of the chair to scrape the floor. "I'll take one day's leave today and send you to see a doctor."

Dr. Linda Quyen (not her real name) adjusts her spectacles. "Mr. Im, your wife is not pregnant. The pregnancy test is negative. She is suffering from pseudocyesis or false pregnancy."

Du-Ho shifts in his chair. "Oh? What's the cause?"

"Perhaps, your wife is harbouring great expectations of conceiving." Dr. Quyen takes off her stethoscope. "Sometimes, this mental state can induce these symptoms." She puts them on the table. "I've also examined her womb – everything is normal except for an old D&C scar."

"D&C? What's that?"

"D&C means dilation and curettage. In layman terms, an abortion or miscarriage."

"What!" Du-Ho jaw drops.

Nhung hears it before she feels it. Harsh air sucked through gritted teeth, a grunt as an arm is raised and the soft swish of a hand slicing the air. *Thwack!* Du-Ho's slap lands on her face, shifting it sideways.

"Who's child were you carrying?" Du-Ho's eyes narrow, thin as a blade of grass. "Your ex-boyfriend's?"

Nhung is lying on a pillow propped against the headboard of the bed and Du-Ho is sitting on the edge, his face tight with tension.

"N-no ..." Nhung's eyes mist with tears as she cups a hand to her cheek. "I-I don't know."

"My God! What do you mean you don't know?" Du-Ho's anger explodes like a hand grenade with its pin pulled. "Were you a hooker before you met me?" His eyes shine like pieces of jagged glass. "Tell me!" When Nhung does not reply, his anger turns to anguish. "I've no choice but to divorce you!" Muscle quivering in his jaw, he leaps to his feet and strides away.

Back to the present ...

I cross my arms over my chest. "So, whose child were you carrying?"

"I don't know – probably one of my regular customers'. I was working at Nui Tuong Café not as a barista, of course, but as a hostess. When Du-Ho told me he was about to be posted here, I resigned and got a job in a regular café. He started courting me and the rest was history."

I look at my watch. "I got to go." I take out the chits in the bin, pull out my wallet to make payment and tip Nhung. "Thanks for talking with me."

***

Sitting at the writing desk in my hotel room, I type "Saigon *gai goi* [social escorts]" in Google on my laptop, trawl out a short list of websites and click open the first. I click "Our Models" on its home page and am whisked to a new page filled with photos of girls, mostly in their twenties. I pick up my mobile phone and dial a number under "Contact us now!"

I transfer my phone to my left hand and hold it to my ear. "Hello? Saigon Angels Escort?" I grasp my computer mouse with my right hand.

"Good evening, Quang speaking. You want to book an escort?"

"I'm browsing your website now." I open a new Google window on the Internet. "Are your photos real?" I key in tineye. com.

"Of course, sir. What you see is what you get. Which escort do you want to book?"

I move the cursor to a photo of a Vietnamese girl with big, twinkling eyes and breasts as big as solo papayas. "I haven't decided yet, all are pretty." I right-clicked the mouse to copy the image address. "Which escort speaks English?"

"All are English-speaking. Which hotel are you staying?"

I paste the image address on tineye.com. "Ngot Moi Resort – I'm afraid it's not girl-friendly." I click search. My jaw drops! On the results page, three websites also have identical images of this so-called escort. I click on the first website. WTF! It's a fashion website in Vietnamese language. The escort's photo is fake.

"You can meet her in the lobby and she can take you to a reasonably priced love hotel nearby." His voice is edged with impatience. "Have you chosen your girl?"

"You sure your photos are real."

"As God is my witness, they're all real."

I repeat the process with another escort's image. "I'm still browsing your photo gallery and each girl's bio." Jesus Christ! I discover another fake photo! "But going to another hotel sounds troublesome."

"For convenience, you can rent another room in the hotel you're in now. On record, my escort will be a registered guest there. But she'll be in your room, of course."

I click on the website shown on the results page of tineye.com. Holy cow! It's a showbiz website. This time, an actress' photo has been abused. "Err, let me check other websites, and I'll call back if I'm interested." I end the call. In my mind's eyes, I see a thug holding a big callused fist to my face for wanting to reject my escort – as ugly as a scarecrow – standing in the doorway.

***

Inside Takashimaya on Le Lai Street, forty-year-old Dae-Jung, a South Korean expat, stands at the entranceway of the ladies section of the changing area. The door of a cubicle swings open and out steps Lanh, aged twenty-three, garbed in a baby-doll black lingerie. She takes several steps towards him in stilettos, her full breasts bouncing slightly. "How do I look, darling?"

Dae-Jung's eyes blink wider. "Lovely, you want to take it?" A tingle skitters from his asshole to his loins.

"Sure, if it pleases your eyes." Lanh turns and waddles away, the cheeks of her butt quivering like jelly.

Five minutes later, the cashier of the department store aims the scan gun at the barcodes on the price tags of two dresses, two skirts, two pieces of baby-doll lingerie, two pairs of silk panties and two pairs of lacy bras, respectively. Dae-Jung focuses his attention on the lighted pole display for the transaction total and yanks out his wallet. He slips out his platinum credit card and hands it over to the cashier. Her assistant bags Lanh's purchases and hands it to her.

"Thank you, darling," says Lanh, wrapping an arm around Dae-Dung's waist.

As Dae-Jung and Lanh stride away towards the counter, the former's mobile phone in his trouser pocket beeps. He takes it out and reads the text message. "Oh shit! My wife's cookery class has been cancelled. She'll be back early. We'll have to do a quickie in the hotel."

The bus rumbles to a stop at the station in Dong Xoai, a small town 100 km north-east of Saigon, its tyres squealing against concrete. Holding a tote bag in one hand and a Nike sports bag in the other, Lanh steps down from the bus and squints from the sunny glare. Emerging from a group of milling people, a man with short-cropped salt-and-pepper hair approaches Lanh, his face as worn and faded as his jeans.

"Lanh, over here." The short wiry man reaches out for her sports bag. "Pass that bag to me." His voice sounds like a growl from a dog suffering from tonsillitis.

"Thanks, *Cha*." Lanh transfers the bigger of two bags to her father. "My goodness, you've lost weight. Is your diabetes under control?" She walks astride her father, his body bent with age, to a battered Toyota Corolla parked under a tree.

Lanh and her *Cha* enter the small living room of his two-room flat, furnished with faded rattan cane furniture that would make an antique dealer envious. She sinks into a chair which creaks under her weight and places the tote bag on her lap.

Cha shuffles on bare feet on the grey cement floor to her room. "I'll put the bag inside."

From the tote bag, Lanh takes out a box with the words "GNC CoQ-10" on its front, a bottle of Korea-manufactured ginseng capsules, a box of bird's nest and two blister strips of medications for benign prostate enlargement, setting them on the glass-topped rattan coffee table.

Cha comes to sit in a rattan chair across Lanh. "Huh? You bought expensive stuff for me again? Why, thank you." He takes the box of GNC CoQ-10, opens it and takes out a folded leaflet.

Linh sits up straight and crosses her legs at the knees. "That product is good for the heart."

As *Cha* is reading the leaflet, Lanh's mobile phone in her tote bag rings. She fishes it out, looks at the screen and rises to take long strides to the kitchen.

"Yes, Mr Dang." She looks out the kitchen window at blocks of drab buildings scattered amidst greenery. "Another booking? But I'm in my hometown." She lowers her voice to a half-whisper. "Overnight? I see, a foreign tourist. Hmm ...okay, okay, bye."

Lanh returns to her former spot on the rattan chair and slips her mobile phone back in her tote bag.

Cha releases an exhale and returns the leaflet to its box. "Lanh," he jerks upright, stabbing her with a glare, "what kind of work are you doing in Saigon?"

"You already know, don't you? I'm a sales assistant in a jewellery store."

"With that kind of salary, you can afford to buy all these products for me? Tell me the truth – are you selling yourself like a whore?"

Cha's phone rings again and she takes it out of her tote bag again and taps its screen. "Yes, Dae-Jung darling?" Her tone of voice is a forced casualness. "Hmmm ... I'm visiting my father. Hmmm ... I see ... sure, see you next week. Bye-bye-darling." She rests her hand on her lap, still holding her mobile phone, and locks her gaze at her *Cha*. "Yes! Yes! Yes!" Hurt swims in her eyes. "I'm a part-time social escort! A whore – as you call it!" She spits the words out like a cobra spewing venom. "Do I have a choice?"

"Lanh, why have you turned immoral?" *Cha* scrunches his face, making the age lines more prominent. "Don't you have any shame?"

"What shame?" Heat shimmers from Lanh's nails to her arms and neck, bleeding into her cheeks. "What did you do after retiring from your clerical job? Selling newspapers by the roadside for five years – earning peanuts! Mum stayed with you in this shabby flat for thirty years! Her marriage to you was not worth it! Whether you like it or not, it's my immorality that's paying your medical expenses and groceries!"

Harsh reality strikes *Cha* on the face and his eyelids close for a moment with a choked sob, a hangdog expression on his face. "Then live your life in whatever way you want." He pauses, lips quivering. "Yes, I've failed as a father – I'm useless! I admit it! I am useless!" Wiping tears streaming down his cheeks with one hand, *Cha* sucks in an inhale and rises to his feet. "I'll set the table for dinner."

Sitting behind a long countertop glass case in Glitter Jewellery Store (not its real name) inside a shopping mall, Lanh scans the shoppers passing the entranceway. *Come! Come inside and buy!* In the glass case in front of her, brooches and pendants glimmer in their black velvet boxes and rows of rings set with precious stones sparkle like fallen stars in hues of blue, green and yellow. After a while, she looks down at the electronic calculator in front of her and jabs a few buttons. *Bah! This month's sales commission is so little. Hope I get a few escort bookings this week.*

Her mobile phone in her pants pocket rings and she yanks it out and answers, "Yes, *Cha*?" Her tone of voice is matter-of-fact.

"Happy birthday, Lanh!"

After her flare-up with her *Cha* a month ago, the subject of her sideline has become taboo and nothing was spoken about it anymore.

"Oh, thank you, *Cha*."

"I'm in a bus on my way to Saigon now. I should be there in

three hours' time. What time does your shift end?"

"Five. But why didn't you inform me earlier you're coming?"

"I wanted my visit to be a surprise, Lanh." "I'll call you when I'm in the mall. We'll eat dinner in a fine restaurant – a birthday treat. We can go anywhere you like."

"*Cha*, please don't waste money – fast food is fine with me. And where're you putting up for the night?"

"I'll be taking the last bus home – the 9 pm bus. Bye." *Cha* clicks off.

Lanh turns her head to face the waitress. "Tempura set," she says, "miso soup and tea." She snaps the menu shut and places it in front of her.

Without looking up from the menu in his hands, *Cha* utters, "Chicken ramen, chawanmushi and Japanese tea."

The waitress, thin like a rake, repeats their orders, collects the menu and goes away.

"Lanh, I've something for you." *Cha* slips his hand into his side pocket and takes out an envelope folded into two. From the envelope, he takes out a cheque and hands it to Lanh. "This is my birthday present to you."

"Huh?" Lanh takes the cheque and looks at the figure on it. "So much? Where did you get this amount?"

"I sold off the flat."

"Then where're you staying?"

"I'm renting a bed in an old folks' home."

"What!" Lanh's eyes widen in shock. "Where?"

"Vui Mong Nursing Home (not its real name) in Phu Giap village."

"Jesus Christ! That's a stinky, filthy place! It's hardly fit for humans!"

"But it's cheap, very cheap." *Cha*'s lips settle into a grim line. "At first, I wanted to bequeath the flat to your brother. But I reckon he can stand on his own feet. I phoned him yesterday, told him not to send me money any more but to start saving to buy his own house." His eyes brim with regret. "I want to make good my failure to you, Lanh."

"Oh *Cha*!" Lanh's lips quiver. "I'm so sorry I scolded you that way."

"I'd like you to take a vocational course, get a different job." *Cha*'s voice is only a choked breath. "But, it's up to you to do whatever you want with the money."

Lanh reaches across the table and holds *Cha*'s hand, her fake eyelashes spiky from tears.

Back to the present ...
I run a finger up and down the condensation beaded on the outside of my near-empty glass. "Is your father still in the nursing home?"

"He has died." Lanh's eyes spark with moisture as her gaze wanders into a faraway stare.   "Before he died, he requested for the simplest burial." She wipes her eyes with one hand. "You want another drink?"

* * *

Inside a cubicle in a *hot toc* [hair salon] in Nguyen Phi Khanh Street, thirty-something-year-old Singaporean tourist, Frankie (a pseudonym) is sitting on a mattress on the floor of a cubicle with legs spread wide apart. Sitting down, big breasts pressed against his chest, Cuc is straddling Frankie, embracing him, her soft curves moulding into the contours of his lean body. Both Frankie and Cuc are in the raw and goose bumps are prickling over their skins as waves of cold air wash over them from the air-conditioner vent at one wall.

"Ooooh, kiss me, darling," Cuc whispers, her breath hot against his ear.

Frankie and Cuc part a few inches, and the former leans forward and locks his lips with the latter's. He traces the full softness of her lips, then explores the recesses of her mouth, and she drinks in the sweetness of his caressing tongue. A tingle crawls from Frankie's lips to his loins. He pulls away and sears a path down her neck and her shoulders. His tongue returns up the same path up to her lips again. Cuc gasps as her tongue slides against his, and they taste each other's warm moistness. After five minutes, they break the kiss.

"I think your time's up, darling." Cuc yawns, opening her mouth wide, and exposing her small teeth and pink tongue. "I slept late last night."

Frankie sees Cuc's tongue and jerks his head back, eyes spanning wider. "Show me your tongue, please."

Cuc sticks out her tongue.

"What's that on your tongue?"

"Only a blister caused by body heatiness, darling."

Frankie disengages from Cuc, stands and takes a few strides to his pants hanging from a hook on a wall. He dips his hand into its back pocket, pulls out his handphone and switches on the torchlight. He returns to his former spot and squats in front of Cuc. "Show me your tongue, Cuc." Cuc sticks out her tongue and Frankie shines a beam of light at it. "I'm damned! That sore is a syphilis chancre! Oh my God, where's the nearest STD clinic?"

Lesser-known Little Japan

9:30 am

I am moseying down an alley in Little Japan, Saigon, after partaken breakfast in a restaurant in Cherry Hotel at Thai Van Lung Street fifteen minutes earlier. The air is crisp and cool and I take big inhales of it. Faded wooden doors, rusting grille scissor doors, dull aluminum shutter doors and shiny steel grille doors – all closed – line both sides of the lane, and at constant intervals, there are potted plants on the sidewalk and white lanterns, green lanterns and red lanterns – a few inscribed with Japanese hiragana – are hanging from wires strung across the cornices of buildings. Occasionally, mopeds and bicycles zip past me as I zig-zag through the matrix of alleys.

As I approach Osaka-West Massage (not its real name) further ahead, four girls garbed in pink *ao dai* uniforms sitting on an upholstered bench seat at the sidewalk rise to their feet shod in kitten heels. Smiling, they wave at me as I pass them. My eyes jolt wider and I do a double-take. Their beige trousers and sand-coloured long pink tunics are made of see-through fabric. I can see their white bras and their white panties through the gaps between the front and back flaps of the tunics. Long flowing shiny black hair frame their perfect faces and two of them are wearing faux pearl necklaces that complement their ivory-white teeth peeking out from luscious lips parted in come-hither smiles. I recall what Thoi Thanh, my scooter tour guide, told me earlier: the dames in Little Japan are mostly prettier than those in those in other entertainment districts.

A tall, curvy girl steps up to me. "Good morning, sir!" Her tone of voice can attract honey bees. "You want a massage?" She offers a laminated piece of paper to me, her varnished finger nails shining in the morning brightness, but I shove my hands into my pocket.

"How much?"

Her lively eyes shine like obsidian in her peach-coloured face. "Only five hundred thousand Dong."

"Is there a happy ending?"

"Yes, if you want it. But for five hundred thousand Dong, massage is done in the open hall. For happy-ending massage, you have to use a private room. Seven hundred thousand Dong. Happy ending is charged separately." She tugs at my wrist with her delicate hand. "Come, sir, non-Japanese are welcome."

I pull my wrist free. "No, thanks."

I continue my walk in a casual and unhurried gait, with my short shadow as my companion.

12:30 pm

Inside a Japanese restaurant, I tuck into a bowl of pork ramen. The broth delivers deep layers of flavours and the ramen offers al dente resistance to my teeth. A bottle of Asahi beer completes my meal.

7:30 pm

I step inside Yokohama Bar (not its real name) and find myself in a hall with a counter bar running parallel to its full length on the right. Behind the bar are a dozen hostesses togged up in tight tank-top uniforms that emphasize their jutting breasts and slim waists. Seven of the girls are engaged in conversation with seven Japanese salarymen respectively, their backs facing me. Shiny bald spots on the back of three heads reflect the ceiling lights.

A forty-something woman, obviously the mamasan, greets me, "*Konbanwa, kauntaba e yokoso.*" A traditional floral print kimono hugs her svelte figure and her hair is tied up in a bun, held in place by a wooden hair pin and decorated with a lacquered red comb with a design of a white crane.

"Huh? No tables in here?"

"This is a Japanese-style counter bar." Mummy's dark penetrating eyes appraise me. "You're not Japanese?"

"No."

"You're still welcomed." Mummy nods. "Come, take a seat at the bar. You can talk to any hostess who's not engaged."

"Who speaks good English?"

"All speak English and basic Japanese." Mummy steps closer to me, puts a hand to the small of my back and nudges me to the bar. A whiff of jasmine from her perfume caresses my nostrils.

I plop down on a high-legged tub chair between a scrawny man and a paunchy man to face a twenty-something hostess sporting a sleek, long bob with side-swept bangs. Wow! The foam cushion of the tub chair is as soft as a cloud which tempts me to stay here as long as possible.

"*Xin chao*! I'm Jackson from Kuala Lumpur." I hold out my hand and my hostess pumps it.

A pair of big lively eyes between high cheekbones in a delicate face holds my gaze. "My name's Lang. What do you want? Sake? Sochu? Whisky? Brandy?" If looks could kill, she'd need a hunting permit for her eyes.

"Sake – Kokuryu, a small bottle." I shift in my seat.

Lang turns and takes a stride to a bar cabinet behind her – its racks and cubbies jammed with bottles and glasses. She returns to her former spot and puts a glass and a 720-ml bottle of Kokuryu Black Dragon in front of me. From under the counter, she takes out a container of ice cubes and a pair of tongs.

The paunchy man gets off his tub chair and his hostess moves along the length of the bar counter to come out. I cast a sideway glance at the potbellied fella and back to Lang. "Can a customer barfine a hostess out?"

Lang opens my bottle of sake and her crimson lips curve into a smile of sweetness and youth. "Jackson, there is no prostitution in this bar." She fills my glass with sake and ice cubes.

My gaze snaps to the paunchy man and his companion climbing up a flight of steps at the back of the hall and then back to Lang. "Can a customer hold a hostess' hands?"

"We've private rooms upstairs."

"For doing what?"

Lang shifts her weight to one foot. "For more intimate conversations."

"Why don't you sit down?"

"We stand while working, sitting is not allowed."

"For eight hours?"

"Yes. And on heels, too."

I scratch the back of my head. "Well, I'll be ..."

Lang and I talk about Vietnamese art and culture for twenty minutes, and the paunchy man and his hostess return to their former spots at the bar. My mouth goes slack! The forehead of the roly-poly – his face wearing a smug expression – is covered with lipstick smudges. His hostess, a long-haired lass, hands him a serviette and he wipes his forehead with it. I lift my sake glass to my lips and Mummy sidles to the space between me and the pot-bellied man and half-whispers to him, "Mr Saito, your fly is undone."

Sake spews from my lips.

11:35 pm

I put some ice cubes into my rocks glass and fill it with sochu till its brim. I am sitting in the karaoke hall of Jujitsu KTV Bar (not its real name). Earlier, a waitress took my order, served my sochu and told me that her mamasan was busy and would come soonest possible. The hall is a full house and bursting at the seams and disco music is in full swing.

Ten minutes pass. Mummy, garbed in a kimono dress, and who looks like somebody's grandmother, clatters on wooden clogs to my table with four hostesses in tow. "Oh, sorry, sir," Mummy says, "to keep you waiting." Her lips zag into a smile. "I'm Mummy Mandy."

The four sex bombs, all togged up in miniskirts and heels, stand a few feet away from me. "*Konbanwa*," they greet me in a chorus.

"Hello," I say, nodding. "I'm not Japanese."

The four girls giggle, and one covers her mouth with her hand.

I flit my gaze across their faces. "Who speaks fluent English? And can tell me interesting stories?"

A girl with shoulder-length hair raises one hand. "Me!" She locks her gaze with mine through small eyes and fans herself with one hand. "Phew, it's hot in here or is it just you?" She smiles, then puckers her kissable lips.

Great balls of fire! My jaw goes slack in surprise. Where did she learn that?

"That's Ping." Mummy Mandy's eyes light up in apparent delight. "She speaks excellent English, loves to talk." Another smile pulls at the corners of Mummy's lips. "She makes excellent company."

I nod at Mummy Mandy and Ping moves in small steps to sit across me. Mummy points a slender finger at our table and hollers at a passing waitress, "Three lady's drinks for Ping! She's going to chat with this customer till the cows come home!"

I extend my arm across the table and Ping holds my hand in a firm grip for a moment. "I'm Jackson." I rest both my hands on the table. "Where're you from?"

"A village near Bac Lieu."

I take a sip of my sochu. "Where's that?"

"A coastal town."

"Any tourist attractions there?"

Ping crosses her legs at the knees, sits straighter and tosses her long hair sideways. "The Bac Lieu Bird Sanctuary and Xiem Cam Pagoda are nearby."

I ask a few questions about the bird sanctuary and the pagoda to break the ice and segue to my main interest. "Tell me everything about yourself and I'll give you a fat tip. Is this your first job in Saigon?"

Ping's eyes dance up to me. "No, I first worked in a cleaning company."

Three years ago ...
Mrs Trang, owner of Trang Kleening Services (not its real name), looks down at a thick book and flits her gaze to the faces of her three female employees, all garbed in blue dungarees and white t-shirts. "Where's An-Dung?"

"Toilet, I think," answers Ping, pushing away a few stray hairs from her forehead.

Aged twenty-two years and sporting shoulder-length curly hair, Ping hails from Bac Lieu, a small town about 200 km south of Saigon.

"Alright, here are today's assignments. Ping, you've two apartments today in Phu My Hung area – standard service; Tracy, washing and ironing; Sang, shopping of groceries, then cleaning of windows at a bungalow in Tan Binh district." She scribbles the tasks on a pad of job sheets, tears each page out one by one and passes them to the girls.

The door in Mrs Trang's office room opens and in steps An-Dung, the dull-eyed van driver. "Sorry, Mrs Trang, I was in the toilet."

Mrs Trang casts a glance at a wall map of Saigon. "Drop Sang first at Lotte Mart, then Ping and Tracy. Go back to pick Sang to deliver the groceries and drop her at Tan Binh district. Then come back and pick me."

Pushing a cart containing cleaning implements, Ping walks down a corridor to search for a particular apartment. She finds it, stops walking and jabs the doorbell. The chestnut-coloured door swings open to reveal a late-thirties Japanese man, dressed in slacks and a t-shirt, standing tall and straight like a bamboo. "Ah, I see that you're from Trang Kleening Services." Dark sharp eyes look out from his narrow face to scrutinize Ping's face and ample chest straining against the cotton fabric of her t-shirt. "Odd, I haven't seen you before."

"I just joined last week." Ping pulls out a sheet of paper from the side pocket of her dungarees and looks down. "You're Mr.

Hiromasa Mikoto (a pseudonym), standard cleaning service for the whole apartment including bathrooms."

"Yes, that's right." The Japanese man steps aside to press his back against one wall. "Enter, please. You are?"

"Tat Ping – Tat is my family name, so call me Ping."

Ping enters the apartment, towing the cart behind her, and Hiromasa closes the door. She finds herself in a marble-floored living room furnished with standard furniture, a TV and a karaoke system. The pigeon-hole shelves on the wooden TV cabinet are filled with CDs, books, a few bonsai plants and a framed photograph of Hiromasa and his wife, a stout bob-haired woman. As Ping starts to vacuum the floor, Hiromasa goes to sit on an L-shaped settee and works on his laptop. After one-and-a-half hours, with nary any word spoken between them, Ping completes her tasks, hands over the job sheet for Hiromasa to sign and leaves.

One week later ...

Inside Hiromasa's living room, Ping lifts up the vacuum cleaner from the cart and puts it on the floor. As she is attaching a curved wand to the hose of the cleaner, Hiromasa steps towards her. "Ping," he says, eyes boring into her, "I've a special request today." His right hand is holding a bundle of cloth.

Without looking at Hiromasa, Ping continues to attach an extension wand to the curved wand and asks, "Yes, sir?"

"Please, call me Hiromasa."

"Yes, Hiromasa?"

"Today, can you wear a Sailor Moon costume while cleaning?"

"Huh?" Surprise jolting her rigid, Ping flicks a gaze at Hiromasa. "Why?" She returns her attention to fixing the floor nozzle to the extension wand.

"I'm an ardent cosplay fan!" Hiromasa's eyes twinkle with apparent desire. "I like Sailor Moon mangas." He offers the bundle of cloth to her. "I'll pay you a big tip."

Ping unfurls the bundle to reveal a one-piece dress consisting of a top with a short sewn-on blue skirt, a front red bow near the bust-line, another back red bow at the hipline, puffy short sleeves and a sailor collar.

"This costume is free-size as the material is stretchable."

"Gee … it's very short and revealing." A wrinkle wedges Ping's small nose. "Err, what happens if your wife comes back suddenly?"

"Don't worry about her." Hiromasa gives Ping a conspiratorial wink. "She teaches conversational Japanese at a language school during the weekends, won't be back until 9 pm."

For the next one-and-a-half hours, Hiromasa's eyes become rounder as he ogles at Ping's creamy butt cheeks and shapely legs while she works, his gaze following her everywhere.

Mouth curved into a smile, Hiromasa swings the front door shut after Ping enters the living room with her cart. As Ping unloads her cleaning implements, he walks with a loose swaggering gait to an armchair facing her and plops down on it, his heart hammering with excitement.

Hiromasa clears his throat. "Ping, I've another special request today." He crosses his legs at the knees.

"This time you want me to wear a Hello Kitty costume?" Ping brings a hand up to her mouth to stifle a giggle.

Hiromasa chortles and the laugh wrinkles at the edges of his mouth become more prominent. "I like your sense of humour!"

He nods. "In fact, I like you very much." He uncrosses his legs and sits straighter. "Today, I want you to work wearing only your undies."

On three past consecutive occasions, Ping has worn the Sailor Moon costume. The first time, she was very embarrassed; second, slightly embarrassed; third, nonchalant.

"Undies?" Ping unloads a bucket from the cart, her gaze trained on Hiromasa. "What's that?"

"Underclothes – bras and panties."

"What!" Ping's rosebud mouth parts in surprise, revealing small white teeth. "Take off my clothes?"

"Yes." Hiromasa's tone of voice is serious.

A look of discomfort crosses Ping's face. "Err, I've my limits."

"I'll give you an even bigger tip compared to the Sailor Moon thing." Hope gnaws in Hiromasa's gut.

Another three weeks later ...

"Hiromasa," asks Ping, wearing a bright-eyed look in anticipation of earning another big tip, "what do you want me to wear today?"

Hiromasa's eyes darken with lust. "Wear nothing and have sex with me."

Heat scalds Ping's cheeks. "I'm sorry, wearing undies is the limit." Ridges furrow her brow as she glares at Hiromasa. "I don't sell sex – please don't pressure me or I'll report you to Mrs Trang."

Hiromasa drops his gaze to the floor and rubs the back of his neck. "In that case, just do your work in your uniform." He plods to the bedroom, flops on the bed and stares at the ceiling with a groan.

The washing machine in Mr. Wolfgang's fifth-floor apartment stops spinning, and Ping opens its side door. As she stoops to transfer clothes from the machine to a rattan basket, her mobile phone in her dungarees side pocket rings. She straightens up, answers the call and moves to the railing of the back balcony where she is standing on.

Ping looks down at the swimming pool on the ground, which appears like the size of an A4 paper. "Yes, *Cha*?"

"Ping! I'm in trouble." The voice is thick and unsteady. "I need money urgently."

"What trouble?" Ping's heart flutters in her chest like the wind through her hair.

"I hit a cyclist with my scooter yesterday. It was my fault as I was drunk. Worse, I didn't have insurance and road tax – both expired a fortnight ago and I forget to renew them. I've agreed to settle this matter privately with the victim. I also broke my ankle and won't be able to work for probably a month. When the victim is discharged from hospital, I've to settle his bill, get him a new bicycle and compensate him for loss of wages."

"Why don't you get the money from *anh trai*?"

"Your brother's contributing something but it's not enough."

Blown by the breeze, stray strands of hair dance about on Ping's face. "Okay, how much do you need?" She pushes them away. "What! So much? My goodness ... If you don't pay up, you may go to jail?" A gush of frustration escapes from her lips. "Alright, I'll think of something." She ends the call and, after taking a few deep breaths to fortify herself, dials Hiromasa's number.

Wearing a shower cap, Ayumi steps out of the bathroom in a state of nature into the bedroom and rubs her feet on the floor mat to dry them. Cold air feathers her stout body, causing goose bumps to rise. She traipses to one wall, takes the air-con remote control off its holder and jabs a button to raise the temperature. Then she aims the remote control at the air-con, presses a button and the former beeps once.

Pulling off the shower cap, she goes to sit at the dresser chair and begins to comb her shoulder-length hair.

Lying on a pillow propped against the headboard, Hiromasa closes the paperback novel and puts it on the side-table. *Sheesh! She wants her weekly sex!* In the dresser mirror, he sees a stout woman with a flat face, a thick back and big, fat arms. He gets up from the bed, stands and takes off his pajamas. With a swing of his foot, he kicks his pajama pants and shirt to the chair at the writing desk. He switches on the side-table lamp, flops spread-eagle on the bed and looks at the ceiling. *If only Ayumi has the body of Ping!*

Ayumi rises from the dresser chair and goes to switch off the ceiling light. With a throaty chuckle, she moves to the bed and throws herself on top of Hiromasa, squeaking the springs of the mattress. A heavy exhale escapes from Hiromasa's lips as her weight knocks his breath out. "Ugh!" He feels his chest almost caving in! Ayumi clamps her mouth on his and, after a space of several heartbeats, reaches down to squeeze his dickie. Then, she rolls off him, clambers down the bed and squats at the side-table. She pulls out a drawer, takes out a box of condoms and opens it.

"Huh?" Ayumi's eyes circle wider in surprise as she looks inside the box. "Only five condoms left? I thought you bought this box only four, five weeks ago."

Hiromasa swallows a lump growing in his throat. *Oh shit!*

I used three to fuck Ping! "Are you sure, darling? I think you've mistaken." He turns his head to face his wife. "Come on, don't let a trivial matter delay our pleasure." He rolls to his side, extends an arm and pulls Ayumi towards him. "Oh, darling, you're as huggable as Doraemon!" He puckers his lips to initiate a kiss. "Ooooh! I love you so much!" Mouth twisted in a humourless grin, he braces himself for another crush from her weight.

Handbag in the crook of her arm, Ayumi steps into a security equipment store and saunters to the left-hand counter where a pony-tailed sales assistant wearing a long-sleeved dress shirt is seated.

"Yes, madam," asks the sales assistant, "how can I help you?"

Ayumi plops down on a stool and puts her handbag on her lap. "I am looking for a spy camera." A gentle aroma from the sales assistant's perfume feathers her nostrils which collide with the grim look in her eyes. "I want to keep an eye on my maid."

"How about a wall clock spy camera?"

"It's for my bedroom. I want to catch my maid rummaging through my drawers."

The sales assistant stoops to open a door at the back of the counter. "Then I suggest a spy camera in a digital alarm clock." She takes out a rectangular black clock measuring about two by three inches in breadth and length respectively and puts it on the counter. "Recording can be played on a PC, no driver needed."

Ayumi takes the clock and examines it. "Motion activated?"

"Yes, of course."

"Can record in the dark?"

The sales assistant points to a pinhole on the clock face. "It has IR, records both video and audio, but the IR light cannot be seen with the naked eye."

"Recording time?

"Six hours, images are of high resolution, thirty frames per second."

Ayumi lifts her handbag and puts it on the counter. "I'll take it." She opens her handbag. "How much is it?"

Two weeks later ...

Ping enters her work place, steps to the punch card machine and takes out her attendance card from the rack. Before she can clock in, Mrs Trang opens her office door and hollers, "Ping, don't bother to punch in – come here!" She closes the door and returns to her desk.

A minute later, Ping is sitting facing her employer. "Yes, Mrs Trang?"

Mrs Trang pulls out a drawer, takes out an envelope and tosses it to Ping. "Here's your letter of termination and one month's pay. As per the contract of employment, there's no severance pay in the event of misconduct."

"What! What misconduct? Please explain, Mrs Trang."

"Cut the pretence!" Mrs Trang's eyes sparkle like jagged emeralds. "You've ruined my company's good name. Mrs Ayumi Mikoto has complained about you! And she has supplied video evidence as well." She rises to her feet and points to the door. "Take your salary cheque and leave!"

Back to the present ...

"After I lost my job, I phoned Hiromasa and told him everything." Ping lifts her shot glass, takes a sip of her lady's drink and her gaze captures mine as she puts down the glass. "He felt guilty about me losing my job. Then he asked me whether I would be interested to work here." She wipes her lips with a serviette. "When I agreed, he sent me for Japanese and English conversational lessons at a language school before introducing me to Mummy."

I stare into the dark brown of Ping's eyes. "What happened between Hiromasa and his wife?"

"Ayumi asked Mrs Trang to send a male cleaner or she would terminate the cleaning contract. My former boss didn't want to lose the business, so she sent Aun-Dung, the van driver." Ping's mouth skews into a wry smile. "Hiromasa was shocked when Aun-Dung showed up in his condo. A year later, Hiromasa's contract ended, and he returned to Japan."

3:00 am

The sky above me is darkness married to a smattering of stars. Lanterns and street lamps scatter illumination on both sides of the drag I am sauntering along. Grille scissor doors, aluminum shutter doors and steel grille doors reflect glimmers of light from the illumination. Pedestrian traffic is a pale shadow of its earlier strength.

Ahead, outside a closed bar, two hostesses, now togged up in jeans and casual tops, are waiting for someone to pick them up. A moped sputters past me, stops at a garbage bin a short distance further down and its rider gets off. He opens the lid, shines a torch inside the bin and starts to rummage through the trash.

Partway back to my hotel, an early twenties street hooker – obviously eager to close a last deal – steps away from her parked scooter on the lantern-lit sidewalk and accosts me. "Mister, you want to fuck me?" she asks.

Taken aback, I jerk ramrod straight as a rash of heat rushes up the back of my neck. "My goodness! You're so vulgar!"

"You want to play with me in bed?" Her voice is as sweet as that of an angel's.

I plough my hand through my hair and, in a lapse of indiscretion, say, "I'm too drunk to fuck."

"My goodness!" she snorts, her lips in a sneer. "You're so vulgar!" Her tone of voice matches her big eyes throwing daggers at me.

* * *

"Mr Matsu, here's your bill." A grin tips the corners of Mummy Hai's lips as she places a platter containing a sheet of paper on the coffee table. "I hope you've enjoyed your evening here."

Seated beside a busty young hostess, Matsu (not his real name) pulls out his fat leather wallet and pulls out a pile of money notes. He looks at the bottom figure on the bill and starts to count the notes.

"Oh darling, my father's water buffalo just died," says the hostess snuggled beside Matsu, one arm coiled around his waist, her thigh touching his. "Can you please help him out?" She smiles, revealing ivory-white, even teeth.

Matsu flicks a side gaze at the hostess. "I'm an old hand at this trick, dear." Smiling, he pats her creamy thigh. "Your father's water buffalo dies every day, huh?" He chuckles as he counts some notes, folds them and slips the wad into her deep cleavage. "Anyway, this big tip will partially cover the cost of a new buffalo."

"Oh, darling, thank you." The hostess disentangles her arm, rises and struts away on stilettos. "Goodnight. Come again."

Matsu pats the empty space vacated by the hostess. "Mummy, please sit down." He nods. "I want to talk with you." He looks at the bill again and places the payment on top of it.

"Yes, Mr Matsu?" Mummy drops her butt on the leather settee which lets out a whoosh.

"Mummy, I'll come straight to the point." Matsu harrumphs. "Can you find me a virgin?"

"Oh? I see. Err, long time or short time?"

"Overnight in a hotel. Zalo to me her photo and the asking price. We'll take it from there" Matsu's smile slides into a smirk. "Of course, I need to see a doctor's certificate of virginity."

Inside his hotel room, Matsu hears the doorbell ring, and he shuffles in room slippers to open it. He blinks, confused. Mummy Hai steps inside, followed by a plump woman in her forties and two muscled bouncers from the nightclub.

"Good evening, Mr. Matsu." Mummy Hai's tone of voice is cold.

"What's going on?" Alarm creeps into Matsu's tone of voice. "Who's this woman?"

"The virgin you booked."

In a flash, one beefy bouncer swings the door shut and bolts it. The other moves to stand beside Mummy Hai and folds his arms over his chest.

"But he's in her forties and is fat! The photo in Zalo shows a slim woman in her late twenties!"

"Sorry, I was deceived myself as a friend introduced her to me." Mummy Hai swallows hard. "I was sent an old photo which I forwarded to you." She pulls out a folded piece of paper from her pants side picket. "Here's the doctor's certificate."

Matsu points a finger at the forties woman. "You're a bloody cheat!"

"She's a roadside fruit-seller," Mummy Hai says, "and doesn't understand English!"

Matsu swings his gaze at Mummy Hai, his eyes sparking fire. "How dare you take me for a sucker?" The muscles in his neck tightens. "I'm not taking her!"

"Say whatever you want – please pay up."

The two brawny bouncers move closer to Matsu and glare at him. Mummy Hai performs liposuction on his wallet and leaves with her entourage.

Two weeks later ...
Mummy Bridgette picks up her mobile phone lying on the desk in front of her. "Yes, Mr Matsu, you received the photo of the virgin and a snapshot of her ID? Plus doctor's certificate?" She leans back in her swivel chair. "Great! As you can see from the numerals on her ID, she was born in nineteen ninety-two." A grin flickers on her lips. "Hmmm ... So, where shall the place be? Okay, text me the room number. Bye."

Matsu opens the hotel-room door as far as the chain lock will allow and peeps out the crack. He sees Mummy Brigitte standing outside with a twenty-something bob-haired girl and a toughie sporting a tattoo on his neck. A tingle surges through Matsu's loins which turns into a vicious pounding. He unhooks the chain look and swings open the door.

Mummy Brigitte steps into the room, leads the bob-haired girl inside and heads straight to the bed. "Sit down." Mummy pulls the bob-haired girl down by the hand. When the latter plonks her bum on the edge of the mattress, Mummy moves towards Matsu, dips into her handbag and produces a folded piece of paper. "Her virginity certificate," she says to Matsu who takes the piece of paper.

Matsu reads the certificate and returns it to Mummy. "So far so good." He moves to stand in front of the bob-haired girl. "What's your name?"

She looks around the room but does not answer.

Matsu's gaze swivels back to Mummy. "Is she deaf?"

"No, a little slow."

Wariness tightens the muscles in Matsu's throat. "What do you mean?"

"Err, mentally retarded."

"What!" Matsu recoils in shock. "That's disgusting!"

"But I've her mother's permission to bring her here."

"Please take her away! I won't do anything illegal!"

"No refund! I've to pay her mother!"

Matsu pulls out his wallet from his trouser back pocket. "Here, take the money and leave." He starts to count some money notes. "I'll use this room to book a social escort." He huffs out a sigh that rattles his lips.

***

Kolkata, India, one year ago ...

Inside a hotel room, Tomoko Ikeda (a pseudonym) picks up his mobile phone and looks at the contact number on a social escort agency's website on his laptop. He leans back in his chair and calls the number. "Hello? Kolkata Desire Escorts?"

"Yes, we are." The voice is gruff and accented. "You want to book our escort?"

"Yes, I do."

Aged fifty-six, Tomoko Ikeda works for a Japanese company in Saigon. He is a widower and his two daughters in Tokyo have married and moved out a few years ago.

"Any particular escort from our website."

"No, but I want a mid-thirties woman, speaks English and is HIV positive."

"What! Is this some kind of joke, sir?"

"I'm serious."

"Why do you want a HIV-positive girl?"

"I want to marry her – with a purpose."

"Go to hell! Don't waste my time with your silly game!"

Click! The line goes dead.

Tomoko phones another social escort agency and makes the same request. Again, his request is rejected. So do the third and fourth agencies he tries. Exasperated, he flips the top of the laptop down, rises from the chair and pockets his mobile phone.

Outside the hotel, he hails a taxi, gets in the back and says to the driver, "Take me to Sonagachi."

"Huh?" The taxi driver jerks upright in his seat. "That's India's biggest red-light district! You sure, sir?" In the rearview mirror, he sees a narrow face with a long hawkish nose, penetrating eyes and salt-and-pepper hair cut short.

Tomoko flicks his gaze from the shafts of light thrown by cars, motorcycles and auto-rickshaws passing by to the back of the driver's head. "Of course, I'm sure!" His tone of voice is solemn.

Tomoko steps into the first floor of a building and finds himself in a hall with five or six woman of various ages watching TV. They mutter among themselves as they stare at him and an ageing pimp – probably in his fifties and dressed in a dhoti – rises from his wooden chair. He approaches Tomoko and stops a few feet away, eyeing him from head to toe.

"You speak English?" asks Tomoko.

The pimp hikes his chin. "*Tum kya chaahate ho?*"

Tomoko forces a smile, pivots on his heels and leaves. He climbs another flight of steps to enter another brothel where the setup is similar: a hall with cubicles running along its length. A young, handsome man with curly black hair accosts Tomoko. "Good evening, sir!" He flashes a toothy smile. "I'm the girls' broker. Come, choose your girl. Only USD300!"

Tomoko bristles at the price. *WTF! Ten minutes earlier, a street hooker proposed only 500 rupees to me for a fifteen-minute remove-panties-only session!* He pauses to suppress his annoyance. "I'm looking for a HIV-positive girl, English-speaking." Tomoko casts a glance at the women sitting outside their respective doorways. "I want to talk with her."

"What!" The young man slaps his forehead with an open palm. "You want to commit suicide by contracting HIV?"

Stepping towards the front end of the corridor, the broker announces something in Hindi at the top of his voice, and his stable of floozies laugh uproariously. One of them puts a forefinger to the side of her head and turns it in a circle a few times.

"Sorry, sir," says the broker, spreading out his hands. "No such girls in here."

Thirty minutes and eight brothels later, Tomoko is tramping down Chittaranjan Avenue, his knees tired from climbing up and down staircases and his heart filled with disappointment. The drag is choked with traffic and pedestrians are streaming along the sidewalk like ants. He stops and looks for a spot where he can hail a taxi.

A hand pats him on the shoulder and he turns to see a thirty-something woman standing a few feet away. Wearing long hair, she is fair-skinned and has on a beige lace blouse and dark pants.

"Excuse me, sir, I'm HIV positive," says the woman, her big eyes shuttering half-way. "I saw you talking to my broker earlier, but I didn't want to reveal my condition at that time." Her thick red lips curl at one side in apparent curiosity. "So, you're HIV positive and want to have unprotected sex, isn't it?"

"No, I'm HIV negative." Displaying a stony expression, Tomoko scratches his long hawkish nose. "Can we sit down somewhere and talk?"

"That's strange." The woman crimps her eyebrows in question. "What's your motive?"

"I want to marry you – it's a sham marriage, of course." A devilish grin eases across Tomoko's face. "I'll pay you a one-time fee, rent you a flat for two months, then we get registered and go separate ways."

"You're not using my name to scam other people, aren't you?"

"Of course not!" Tomoko stares as if she has flicked food on his face. "I'm an expat from Saigon, a business executive." He pulls out his wallet from his trouser side pocket. "Here's my name card." He slips out a business card and hands it over to the woman. "I'm Tomoko Ikeda, originally from Tokyo."

The woman looks down at the card. "I'm Madhuri." She points to a doorway glowing with lights further ahead. "We can sit in that restaurant."

Two months later ...

"What's your problem," asks Dr. Gupta (not his real name) leaning forward to read the patients' names on the card in front of him, "Mr Tomoko Ikeda and Mrs Madhuri Ikeda."

Tomoko swings his gaze to Madhuri seated beside him and back to the doctor. "We got married recently so we want a HIV test before we start a family." He pulls out his marriage certificate from his pocket, unfolds it and places it in front of him.

Two hours later, Dr. Gupta says, "Mrs Madhuri Ikeda, I'm afraid you're HIV positive, but your husband is negative."

"Oh my God!" Tomoko feigns a shocked look and holds his wife's hand. "In that case, can you give me a prescription for a PreEP drug?" His tone of voice is tinged with an excitement which collides with his worried expression.

"Sure, I can give you a prescription for Tenvir-EM. That's the generic version of Truvada." Dr. Gupta removes his stethoscope hanging from his neck, places it on his desk and leans forward. "But you need another test to determine that you are medically fit to take the drug."

Little Japan, Saigon

The curtain of the doorway of Yokubo Nightclub (name changed) parts and the lean and tall figure of Tomoko swaggers in. Mummy Jennifer and a waitress holding a menu are waiting several strides away.

"Hello, Tomoko Ikeda-San!" Mummy Jennifer steps forward and bows, her lips upturned in a smile. "Long time no see! You must never forget an old friend like me!" Her smile blooms into a grin. "I just recruited three new girls last week. Ooooh ...they're your taste."

Mummy Jennifer swivels on her heels and escorts Tomoko down a corridor to the VIP Karaoke Room. As their heels click on the marble floor, romantic vibes sizzle in the nightclub as Hikaru Utada's voice croons out a slow love song from speakers.

Inside the plush karaoke room, Tomoko plonks his tight butt on the settee. "Mummy, I've a special request tonight."

"Yes?" Mummy arches her eyebrows.

"After I've selected my hostess for barfine, can you pull her aside and ask whether she can have unprotected sex?"

"What!" Mummy gapes in shock. "You're not afraid of contracting HIV?"

Chuckling, Tomoko pulls out a bottle from his side trouser pocket. "See?" He rattles the bottle of Tenvir-EM. "I've got anti-AIDS drugs ready!"

"But why should any girl want to do it raw with you?"

"Here're my HIV test results for the past three months. All negative." Tomoko pulls out a folded piece of paper from his shirt pocket. "Here, when you talk to your girl, show her these laboratory results." He hands over the paper to Mummy Jennifer. "And, of course, I'll pay a premium for her services." He raises his eyebrows. "Not to mention a fat tip for you!"

"Oh, you're a genius, Ikeda-San!" Mummy Jennifer holds the paper in one hand but does not bother to look at it. "You've covered your ass both ways!" Her hand flies to her mouth. "Ooops! I meant that in a good sense."

Back to the present ...

"In America, Truvada costs around USD1,800 for a bottle of 30 tables." Tomoko re-fills his porcelain cup with sake from a black ceramic bottle. "Tenvir-EM is sold in India at only 1,200 rupees – that's roughly USD18." Leaning forward, he tops up my cup with sake and his facial muscles tighten. "PreEP drugs are also pricey, very pricey, in Japan." He relaxes his expression. "So that's why I fly regularly to India to get my supply." He puts the ceramic bottle back on the table.

I take a sip of my sake. "You smuggled the drug in inside your suitcase?"

A grin cracks Tomoko's face. "No need to smuggle! You can bring PreEP medicine into Vietnam with a prescription as long as it's for personal use."

"Holy sweet angels ..." I scratch at my chin. "What a progressive liberal country. Gay Pride parade is allowed; PreEP is also allowed to be brought in."

Paddy Fields, Buffaloes and Rats

The rumble of the engine in the FUTA express bus sounds like a muted drone of a motorboat. I am reclining on a sleeper chair with my eyes closed but I am not asleep and a baseball cap is jammed over my head as the gust from the overhead air-conditioning vent is a tad too cold – for me at least. I feel the bus slow, swerve to the left and come to a halt.

A pudgy hand pats me on the shoulder. "Jackson, we've arrived at the bus station," says Thanh's voice from across the aisle between us.

Four hours earlier, we left Mien Tay Terminal at Kinh Durong Vuong in downtown Saigon. Three days ago, I met Thoi Thanh (name changed) when I rode her scooter on two separate tours. First, it was a customized nightlife tour as described in *Pattaya Undercover (Includes Bangkok, Saigon and KL)*, followed by a foodie tour in the evening the next day. After having gotten acquainted with her, I sealed a deal to visit her home village in the outskirt of Hong Ngu. The latter is a riverine town located 180 km west of Saigon.

Opening my eyes, I see cherubic-faced Thanh picking up her plastic bottle of water from the rack at the back of the seat in front of her. "Who's meeting us?" I ask.

Thanh upends the bottle, makes loud gulping noises drinking the water, and replaces it in its former spot. "My sister." In her late twenties, squashed-nosed Thanh is wearing an ear-length bob with bangs and a pair of dark pants paired with a beige crew-neck t-shirt. Her hairstyle makes her face resemble a puffer fish.

Wearing a pointed conical straw hat, I cycle behind Thanh who's leading on her bicycle. Seemingly interminable expanses of paddy fields embosom both sides of the drag. Copper hues from the rising sun bath down on us and create grey silhouettes of trees, coconut palms and shrubs dotting the drag. The morning breeze tousles my hair and carries with it the fragrance of the earth. Second by second the sky is becoming brighter.

After pedalling for almost ten minutes, Thanh turns left to descend to an earth road and, after cycling some distance, turns left again. We are now on an elevated bund traversing one end of a paddy field to another which seemingly converges with the now bluish sky. Though I need more effort to pedal my bicycle on the hard earth than before, the red-cotton trees and Callery-pear trees dotting the bund ignite an inner smile in me with their red and white five-petalled blossoms.

Thanh stops cycling and leans her bicycle against a red-cotton tree. "Let's wait here," she says, casting her gaze at a Kubota harvester parked at a spot about a hundred metres to our right. I stop cycling, prop my bicycle on its side stand and sit down next to Thanh. We talk shop and, after a while, a group of about a dozen boys and an early thirties man come in our direction. Garbed in dark shorts and white shirts, the boys are all carrying jute bags with drawstrings and the man has a clipboard jammed under one armpit. Behind them are two farmers in shabby work clothes.

As they pass us, the smartly dressed man and Thanh say something to each other in Vietnamese language. The entourage then proceed ahead to the harvester.

"That man's Mr Khac Nhan (name changed), a teacher. In this village, he has a reputation as a *con trai hoang đàn* – I'll explain the meaning of those words when I tell you his story later." One farmer climbs into the cab of the harvester and another climbs on its side and Thanh continues, "They're going to start the harvest." She flicks a momentary side gaze at me and points to the boys, now separated into two groups. "Teacher Nhan has organized a rat-catching competition for his pupils. He'll give a small reward to the winning group – he does this every harvesting season."

With a rumble, the harvester moves in a straight line, its cutting bars on the gigantic front reel slicing paddy stalks and a feeder moving them up to a thresher. At the bottom of the thresher, a man perched on a platform is filling up rice in sacks, tying them and tossing them to the ground. The boys run behind the harvester – one group on each side – which is dropping paddy stalks from its back chopper. Frequently, they scramble to the ground to catch rats with their hands and toss them into their bags. The harvester finishes four straight parallel routes and is still continuing to move.

"Come," says Thanh, getting up, "let me show you around the village."

We ride our bicycles back to the metalled road and, after thirty minutes, enter a village, consisting of a main drag crisscrossed by several side alleys. We park out bicycles near a lamp-post and start to walk. Along the tree-lined drag, amongst a cluster of zinc-roofed and clay-roofed single-storey houses, there is an aroma-filled coffee shop abuzz with people chattering and eating *pho*; a provisions store where mangoes, dragon fruits, papayas and an assortment of veggies are displayed in rattan baskets on its cement sidewalk; a blacksmith's grey-walled workshop where its owner is sharpening a pair of shears on a block of whetstone; a bicycle-and-moped repair workshop with spanners and screwdrivers strewn on its grease-splattered floor; a potter's workshop where a man is kicking at a fly wheel to keep a turntable spinning while he shapes a vase from a mass of clay placed on top of the latter; and an apothecary's store selling herbs, dried insects, snake wine, dried lizards and bear's gallbladder wine.

As I stand inside the herbal store to browse the displays, the wizened apothecary, probably in his sixties, and Thanh conduct a brief verbal exchange in Vietnamese language. Then Thanh and I proceed ahead along the sidewalk. "That apothecary, Mr Kieu Nam, also doubles as a shaman when necessary," Thanh says. "Not so long ago, river fishing was a dangerous activity. Whenever a fisherman did not return – presumably drowned – and his body could not be found, the apothecary-turned-shaman would make a mulberry-wood statuette and conduct a ritual. Its purpose is to recall the deceased's spirit to reside in the statuette so that a proper burial could be conducted – using the statuette as a surrogate for the missing dead body."

We proceed further on, passing the last few stores and stepping into sunlight. After about a hundred metres, the end of the drag vaguely ends and degenerates into a short, pebbled stretch and we reach a massive pond with its surface sporadically covered with lotus plants. Shady trees fringe the grassy bank of the pond and a water buffalo is grazing under one tree. A man is wading knee-deep in the shallow end of the pond and collecting lotus-flower pods which he deposits into a cane basket strapped to his back.

"I want to pose with a water buffalo!" I fish out my mobile phone from my back jeans pocket and hand it over to Thanh.

"Can you take a photo for me?"

I move to a spot about two feet away from the grey beast, its curved horns probably spanning three feet, its shoulder rising to about four feet high. It appears friendly and merely looks at me with its big eyes, so I move closer to stand beside it.

"Smile!" Thanh clicks on my mobile phone. "One more shot! This time sit on its back!"

"Sure, it won't bite?"

"Of course not!" Thanh chortles. "Water buffaloes are friendly creatures."

I pat the buffalo on its head with an open palm a few times so as not to alarm it. Then I grab the top of its shoulder, climb on its back and sit straight, my legs straddled wide apart.

"Ready? Smile ..." Thanh moves a few steps to her right to get a better angle.

At that moment, the lotus-flower pod collector emerges from the pond, goes to his motorbike parked nearby and kick-starts the engine a few times.

Piak! Piak! Piak! The motorcycle misfires trice! Startled by the loud noise, my buffalo jerks its head up, bellows and starts to run! I am nearly thrown off balance and my hat falls off.

"Eiiiiyah!" Eyes widened in shock, I lean forward and grab the buffalo's horns. "Stop! Stop him! Stop him!" My heart hammers in my rib cage.

"*Dung lai!*" Thanh hollers. "*Dung lai! Dung lai!* Oh, my God!"

Hoofs thudding, the buffalo races down the main drag – kicking up dust – where cyclists, pedestrians and motorcyclists gawk, point at me and laugh, their mouths gaping. After giving me a bum-jarring twenty-second ride, the animal slows down and I release its horns to fall sideways off its back to the ground. Moments later, the lotus-flower pod collector arrives on his motorbike with Thanh riding pillion to where I lay sprawled on the ground.

Thanh hops off the motorbike and runs to me. "Are you alright?"

Grimacing, I lumber to my feet and brush dust off my jeans. "Tssssk … Ouch … I'm bruised in a few places, but luckily, no broken bones."

"Come, let's go to the medicine-man's store." Thanh holds my right upper arm to steady me. "I'll buy you a bottle of bear gallbladder wine – you've to apply it to your bruises."

Mr Thoi rises and lifts up a bottle of rice wine. "Jackson, *bạn se o viet nam bao nhieu ngay?*" He leans across the round dining table and fills my glass with rice wine.

Thanh, sitting beside me, interprets, "My *Cha* asks how long will you be in Vietnam?" Using a pair of steel tongs, she deposits some ice cubes into my glass of rice wine.

I hold up ten fingers. "*Muoi ngay.*"

"*Bạn da xem mot chuong trình mua roi nuoc?*" Mr Thoi sits down, fills his own glass with rice wine and replaces the bottle in its former spot.

Thanh swings her gaze from her *Cha* to me. "Have you seen a water puppet show?"

"No, err, how to say, oh … *khong!*"

Mr Thoi raises two thumbs-ups. "*Dung bo lo no.*"

From the kitchen, Thanh's sister – as plump as her sibling – delivers a plate of lotus roots and a platter of crispy pancakes to the table. "More dishes coming up quickly."

"While waiting for the food, let me tell you the story of Mr Khac Nhan," Thanh says to me.

"*Giao vien Khac Nhan*?" Mr Thoi makes a face and slaps his forehead with an open palm.

Mrs Thoi appears at the table, deposits a bowl of soup in the centre, says, "*Canh Chua*" and goes away.

Then Thanh begins her story ...

Thirteen years ago ...

Hunched over his writing desk in his room, eighteen-year-old Khac Nhan's crotch clenches as he reads a vivid paragraph of an erotic novel. Outside the window of the room, the air is pungent with the fragrance of jasmine and, in the distance, there is an occasional traffic but far away enough not to bother him.

"Nhan! There's a letter for you!" His *Ma* calls from the living room.

Nhan snaps the novel shut, hides it in the drawer of his desk and opens the bedroom door. "Yes, *Ma*?" Stepping into the living room, he combs his fingers through his hair.

"The postman rang trice, and you didn't hear him?" *Ma* hands him an envelope and returns to the kitchen.

Nhan tears open the envelope, pulls out a letter and reads it. "Yippee!" He bolts to the kitchen. "*Ma*, the university has accepted my application!"

"Oh, I'm so happy!" The creases at the corner of *Ma*'s eyes deepen as she smiles. "Looks like you're going to be the first person in this village to graduate from a university!"

"I've to leave for Saigon in two weeks' time." Nhan punches the air with a fist. "I'm going to tell Chau the good news."

Three months later ...

Khac Danh lets his bicycle roll on its own momentum as he approaches the rice mill – a plank structure with a zinc roof – that Chau works in. A short distance from its entrance gate, he dismounts and waits, the evening sun casting his shadow long on the grassy ground. At 5:10 pm, he sees Chau cycling out of the gate entrance and waves at her.

Chau stops cycling, dismounts and pushes her bicycle to stop a few feet away from him. "Mr Khac, what brings you here?"

"Actually, I am just passing through, so I decided to stop briefly regarding a letter from Nhan." Mr Khac pulls out a folded piece of paper from his shirt pocket. "I received this letter yesterday." He unfolds the paper and hands it over to Chau. "What does it say?"

Chau takes the letter and reads it. "He says he's fine and is studying hard." She flicks her gaze up at Mr Khac for a moment. "He hopes that *Cha* and *Ma* are in good health." She continues to read. "He also asks for additional money so that he can buy a bicycle."

Mr Khac squishes his brows. "Huh? Why?"

"Let me finish the letter, Mr Khac." Chau looks down at the bottom of the letter and then re-folds it in two. "He says that his dormitory is far from the different buildings where the lecture rooms are housed. In fact, the campus is spread over four hectares." She hands it back to Mr Khac.

"I see." Mr Khac scratches the back of his head. "Where am I going to get the additional money?" He tosses a faraway look at several birds flying home. "Looks like I've to sell my pigs which have not reached maturity." He releases a sigh and looks back at Chau. "But what choice do I have?" He pauses a tick. "By the way, did he write to you?"

"Yes, I also got a letter from him yesterday." Chau's mouth seems to caress the words as they roll from her lips. "Both our letters were probably posted on the same day."

"Please write a reply for me. Tell him I'll send him a money order as soon as possible." Pain seem to flick across Mr Khac haggard features. "You can sign it on my behalf. I'll reimburse the postage later."

Chau gives a gentle shake of her head, her lips lifting in a gentle smile. "No need to reimburse me."

Another two months pass ...

Mrs Khac raises two coarse fingers. "I heard that Nguyen's water buffalo gave birth to twins!" She whips out a fan from a cloth belt tied around the folds of fat surrounding the area where her waist once was.

"What!" Chau's eyes jolt wider in surprise. "Twins are rare."

Mrs Khac unfurls the fan. "He says he'll have a small celebration for this windfall." She waves the fan at her own face. "He invited us."

Mrs Khac and Chau are sitting on a wooden bench in the former's front porch, a zinc roof propped up by two termite-eaten wooden posts.

"Too bad my parents don't know him that well, that's why we were not invited."

Leaning on the wooden back rails, Mrs Khac slips one foot off a sandal. "Won't you stay for dinner?" She wriggles her toes.

Before Chau can reply, Khac Danh steps out of the doorway into the front porch. "Here, Chau," he says, handing over a piece of paper to her, "this is another letter from Nhan." He stands a few feet from his wife and folds his arms over his chest.

Chau takes the letter, reads it and flits her gaze to Mrs Khac. "More or less says the usual things – he's studying hard, hopes the pigs are growing fat and the hens are laying plenty of eggs." She scrunches her face. "This time he's asking for an additional ten million Dong so that he can buy a laptop."

"Huh!" Khac Danh's jaw drops. "So much?"

Mrs Khac exhales a noisy sigh of frustration. "Is a laptop necessary?"

Chau blinks. "Odd, I did not receive any letter from Nhan this month."

Khac Danh shifts his weight to one foot. "Tell him not to buy unnecessary things." He plants both hands on his hips.

"He says a laptop is an absolute necessity."

"Looks like I'll have to sell my two gold bracelets." Mrs Khac's face twists in anguish. "They were passed to me by my late mother as heirlooms." Two tears slither down her cheeks.

Wearing a hangdog expression, Khac Danh squats on his knees, casts his gaze at the pitted cement floor and shakes his head. "I never expected Nhan's university education to be so expensive." He scrubs a callused palm over his weather-beaten face.

"Mr Khac, I'll help you out this time." Chau sits up straighter. "I'll contribute something."

"Oh, Chau," says Mrs Khac, drying her eyes with her sleeve. "You'll make such a good future daughter-in-law for us!"

Khac Danh wipes away tears of joy and says to Chau, "Chau, maybe you would like to follow me to Saigon when we've the money."

Silk-factory owner, Mr Que hears a rap on the chipboard partition of his cubicle and looks up from the ledger he's writing on in front of him. "Yes?" he asks his young male worker standing in the doorway.

"Sir, there is a Miss Luu Chau outside to see you."

"Huh? The rice mill clerk?" Mr Que puts his pen down on the desk. "Show her in."

He closes the ledger and pushes it to one side.

The young man disappears and Chau steps into the small room. She is garbed in a brown skirt ending below the knees and a long-sleeved floral-print dress shirt.

Mr Que motions a hand in the direction of the visitor's chair. "Please take a seat." He clears his throat after Chau has plonked down. "Yes, Miss Luu, how can I help you?"

"I want to weave silk part time here."

"I don't quite understand. You've left the rice mill?"

"No, I'm still working there. I want to earn additional income – for perhaps two months." Chau's eyes are filled with anticipation. "I can come here in the evening after my work at the rice mill."

Mr Que clasps his hands and rests them on top of his desk. "But we'll be closed. I cannot assign my men to come open and lock the doors just for you."

"Please try to help me." Chau leans forward, her eyes pleading for understanding. "I've an unexpected expenditure and need money urgently."

Mr Que strokes his chin and considers for a moment. "Do you know how to operate a loom?"

"I can learn." Chau's voice edges with excitement. "And I'll weave you the best possible silk."

"Alright, come tomorrow around this time. I'll ask a worker to teach you how to use the loom. Then I'll lend you one loom for two months – excludes its transport to your house and its return to me. You can do the weaving at home. But if you damage the loom, you'll be held responsible, okay?"

"Oh, thank you, sir."

Mr Que picks up a notepad and his pen. "Now, let's discuss your piece-rate wages."

Saigon

The door of Fallen Angels Bar (not its real name) in Bui Vien Street swings inward and in steps a young man, just out of his teens. Mummy rises from her usual spot at the far end of the bar counter when she recognizes Nhan. *Ah! It's that university student again. He must be from a rich family, otherwise how can he afford to come here regularly?* Mummy waddles her big butt on wedges shoes to receive Nhan. "Good evening, Mr Khac Nhan!" She thrusts an open palm in the direction of a booth nearby, swinging the tiny bells on her gold bracelets. "You must come more often! All study and no play makes Khac Nhan a dull boy!" She chuckles to reveal horsey teeth and then puts two fingers to her lips and whistles. *Tweet! Tweet!* A young sex bomb in a red miniskirt and a black halter top emerges from the back of the hall and struts in stilettos towards Mummy who says, "Tracy, your lover boy is here! Go get the menu."

Nhan spoons some rice into his mouth and starts to chew. "Xuan," he says with his mouth full, "can you lend me your bicycle? It's for only a day."

Sitting across Nhan, Xuan takes a gulp of water. "Why?" He

spears a piece of braised yam and pops it into his mouth.

"My father's coming to visit me." Nhan takes a swallow. "I need to show him the bicycle I purportedly bought."

Nhan and Xuan are eating lunch in the canteen of the university they are studying in. Three weeks ago, Nhan received the laptop monies he asked for via a money order together with a letter stating his father will be coming to Saigon at the end of the month.

Xuan swings his gaze at a gorgeous student walking past their table and back to Nhan. "What do you mean by 'purportedly bought'?"

"Please don't bother with the details." Nhan clucks his tongue in irritation. "I just need to show him a bicycle otherwise I'll be in trouble." He pauses, gaze thinning. "You also know anyone who can lend me a laptop? This morning, I asked Hwa to lend me hers but she refused. That snooty bitch!"

"No problem with the bicycle, buddy." Xuan de-shells a prawn with his hands. "Andrew has a laptop and I can borrow it from him." He licks his fingertips.

"Thanks! I'll treat you to a couple of beers in Fallen Angels Bar!" Nhan traces an hour glass with his hands. "The girls there are hot!" He lowers his voice a decibel. "Our course-mates are ugly ducklings compared to them!" He chortles.

Khac Danh enters the visitor's lounge of the university's Residential Hall wearing a conical hat, faded brown long-sleeved shirt and dark baggy trousers tied at the ankles. A towel is wrapped around his neck and a cloth bag is hanging from the crook of his bronzed arm. He takes a seat on a settee and waits, his eyes roving the setup.

At the appointed time as stated in his father's letter, Nhan enters the visitor's lounge with a dark rectangular bag and goes to sit beside him. "Oh *Cha*! Why are you dressed like this? Sheesh! You look like a farmer!"

"What do you mean? I *am* a farmer!" Danh dips his hand inside the cloth bag and takes out a packet wrapped in banana leaves and old newspapers. "Here, your *Ma* made some rice cakes for you." He takes out an envelope. "Here's the money order for next semester's fees."

"Oh, thank you Cha." *WTF! Who wants to eat rice cakes? This is peasants' food!* Nha puts the rectangular bag on the coffee table, unzips it and takes out a laptop. "This is the laptop I bought."

"I see." Danh blinks. "Where's your bicycle?"

"It's outside." Nhan replaces the laptop back into its bag. "Come, I'll show you." He rises, slips the strap of the bag over one shoulder and exits the visitors' lounge.

Danh follows Nhan to a shed where a line of bicycles is parked. Nhan stops at a bicycle with low handles, unlocks the wheel lock and pushes it out of the line. "I bought this mountain bike – it's made by Saigon Cycles."

Danh holds the handles, squeezes the brakes and nods in approval. "This is a good bicycle." He steps away from the bicycle and Nhan parks it in its former spot.

"Can I take somewhere for a bite?" Nhan points a finger in a certain direction. "There are several food stalls nearby."

"I'm taking the 4 pm bus back. Make it a quick meal."

Several months later ...
The young postman stops at the gate of Khac Danh's house, rings

the bell and pulls out an envelope from a stack on his front carrier.

Wearing an apron over frumpy clothes, Mrs Khac goes to the gate to take the letter from the postman who says, "Returned letter."

"Huh? From who?"

The postman adjusts his peaked cap. "Your husband's letter to Khac Nanh at his university."

"What!" Mrs Khac's eyes bug wider. "Why?"

"Very likely he's not staying at the campus anymore." The postman kicks at the ground to reverse his bicycle and pedals away.

Riding her bicycle back from work, Chau reaches her house to see Mr Khac Danh waiting for her under the front porch.

"Yes, Mr Khac," asks Chau, getting off her bicycle, "is anything the matter?"

"Something's amiss! My letter to Nhan has been returned."

Chau's jaw drops. "What!" She props the bicycle on its side stand.

Khac Danh takes out a folded envelope from his shirt pocket. "I'm going to Nhan's university to find out what has happened." He unfolds the envelope and hands it to Chau. "Do you want to go with me?"

"Of course!" Chau takes the envelope and looks at it. "There's a remark which says 'moved'. He's no longer staying there." She returns the envelope to Khac Danh. "But why didn't he inform us?" She huffs out a sigh. "His letters to me has been irregular over the past several months."

Mr Trach, Student Affairs Officer, looks down at the file in front of him and flicks his gaze up at Khac Danh and Chau sitting across his big desk. "Mr Khac, your son Nhan failed four subjects and scraped through two subjects in the first-year finals. So, he had to repeat those."

"What!" Khac Danh stares, the air in his throat thick with shock. "I am not aware of this."

Mr Trach looks down at the file again. "Then last month, he was expelled from Residential Hall."

Chau jerks upright. "Reason?"

"He broke curfew hours frequently, even came back drunk twice and threw up in the corridor on both occasions. Then, he submitted a letter to terminate his studies."

"But, where is he now? He did not return home." Khac Danh holds his hands together in a gesture of appeal. "Please, help us to locate him."

Mr Trach considers for a moment and rises from his chair. "His former room-mate may be able to help you." He goes to a filing cabinet, pulls out another file and opens it. "His name's Nguyen Xuan," he says. "I'll arrange for you to meet him this evening."

The next morning, Khac Danh and Chau are sitting in a pizza chain restaurant and sipping coffee after having spoken with Nguyen Xuan yesterday evening. Their faces are glum and their lips grim. Outside, a pizza delivery boy on a motorbike stops at a reserved parking lot at the road shoulder, gets off the machine and starts to stride towards the restaurant.

Through the glass portion of the front wall, Chau spots the pizza delivery boy and points at him. "Oh my God! Xuan's right! That's Nhan! He's now a pizza delivery boy!"

Nhan takes off his helmet, pushes the glass door inward and steps inside.

"Nhan!" hollers Khac Danh, rising to his feet.

Hair dishevelled, Nhan turns to look at the caller and his face blanches. He turns on his heels and takes urgent strides to leave the restaurant but his father hurries after him. "Nhan, come back! You can't run away from your problems!" On the sidewalk, Khac Danh grabs his son's hand and turns him around.

Nhan drops his gaze at the concrete sidewalk and remains silent.

Khac Danh grabs a fistful of his son's shirt front. "Xuan told us everything! How could you spend our hard-earned money on bargirls?" Fury turns his face ruddy and his eyes glitter like pieces of broken glass. "Do you know that Chau wove silk part-time to contribute something every time you asked for extra money?" Khac Danh's anger turns to hurt and he releases Nhan and mauls his own face with a gnarled hand, "W-Where did I go wrong in bringing you up?" His voice comes in hoarse rasps.

A sob rises in Chau's throat as she forges forward to Nhan, tears sparking her eyes. "How could you do this to me?" She swings her arm and slaps him on the face as hard as she can, shifting it sideways. "I gave you all my love!" she splutters, the pain in her heart bleeding in her voice. "And I trusted you!"

Blinking, Nhan rubs his jaw, opening and closing it a few times to make sure it still works. "I'm sorry, Chau!" Tears brim in his eyes. "I really am and I regret what I've done." He wipes his tears away with his sleeve. "I'll repay your money by monthly instalments. Just tell me how much?" He sinks to his knees and turns his head to face his father. "*Cha*, please forgive me ..." His tone of voice is pregnant with contrition.

Back to the present ...

"His father asked him to quit his job as a pizza delivery boy. So, Khac Nhan returned home and worked on the farm for a few months. Later, he enrolled in a teacher-training school and became a teacher. This morning I told you that Nhan has a reputation as a *con trai hoang đàn*, isn't it? Well, you should know what that phrase means – a prodigal son."

I take a sip of my rice wine. "What about Chau?"

"Oh, Chau forgave him and they got married, eventually."

Carrying an aluminum platter with a cover, Mrs Thoi comes to the dining table, stands in the space between me and Thanh and announces, "Everybody, the main dish is here!" Leaning forward, she puts the aluminum platter on the table and lifts the cover, infusing the dining room with the smoky aroma of grilled meat.

My eyes almost double in size from shock. "Eeeeeeek!" I grab at my throat with one hand. "Yucks!"

Lying on the platter are six rats grilled to a golden brown and sprinkled with sesame seeds.

A giggle bubbles from Thanh's thick lips. "Courtesy of Mr Khac Nhan!"

***

Dung takes a glug of his beer from his stein mug. "How was your trip to Saigon, Thuc?" He slams the mug down on the wooden table and wipes froth from his upper lip with the back of his hand.

"Great!" Wearing a crew cut, Thuc grins and picks up his cigarette from the ashtray. "A *xe om* [motorcycle taxi] took me a pickup spot." He takes an inhale, returns the cigarette to the ashtray and puffs out smoke rings.

Country bumpkins Thuc and Dung, both in their mid-twenties, are sitting in the village coffee shop where cicadas, katydids and crickets are stridulating in the darkness outside. Only two other tables are taken up by oldsters drinking tea.

Dung fingers the condensation on the side of his mug. "I heard that Bui Vien Street and Pham Ngu Lau Street have many girls."

"Sheesh! Those places are for tourists. Very expensive!" Thuc makes a face and shakes his head. "Not worth the price. Le Tuan Mau and Kinh Duong Vuong in District 6 and Hong Bang in District 5 cater more to locals and are cheaper."

Dung slaps at a mosquito at his leg. "Where did you go for your fling?"

"On that night, the *xe om* took me to Hoa Binh Park. Whoopee! There were so many night butterflies waiting there. I struck a deal with a girl who rode a bicycle!" Thuc chortles, revealing crooked teeth. "Then I cycled her bicycle to her room nearby, and she sat on the back carrier!" He laughs uproariously. "Next month, I'm meeting my wholesaler again. Why don't you follow me to Saigon? Have some fun there."

"I can't." Dung looks around as if making sure no one is eavesdropping. "I cannot afford to be naughty so I masturbate," he says in a lowered voice.

"Sheesh! That's a boy's cheap thrill!" Thuc pours more beer into his mug. "Why don't you buy a motorised masturbator? There's a store in Saigon selling such toys – under the counter, of course. I'm not talking about those old-fashioned toys that are designed like torchlights. Today's latest masturbator is like a woman's butt with a pussy." He extends his hands and spreads his fingers in a curled position to form the shape of a buttock. "The latest models are motorised and are replicas of famous Japanese porn stars' pussies." One side of his lips quirk upward. "Each set comes with a print photograph of the porn star. Signed by her! Of course, endorsement by the porn star means the product is expensive. However, that store sells China-made imitations. I can get one for you." He leans forward slightly to Dung. "Just between you and me, I also have one myself."

"Sure, that'll be great." Dung's eyes twinkle with glee.

"From what I recall from seeing their catalogue, they've replica pussies of Haruka Hatano, Azumi Sasaki ... err ... and Suzuka Sakura (all names are pseudonyms) – that's all I can recall. So, whose do you want?"

"Wow! I'm a fan of Suzuka Sakura! Can you get hers for me?"

"Sure." Thuc lifts his mug to take a deep swallow of his beer. "Can you give some part payment first? When I pass you the product with the receipt, we can settle the difference."

"No problem." Dung shifts his hip, shoves his hand into his side trouser pocket and fumbles for his wallet.

Inside his bedroom, Dung closes the wooden louvred window and switches on the ceiling fan. Sitting on the edge of his bed, he opens the seven-by-seven-inch box given to him by Thuc earlier.

"I've asked the seller to insert the batteries so I could test it in the store," Thuc explained. "There was a whirring sound when I pressed the green button, so it works."

Dung takes out a postcard-size photo of Suzuka Sakura in the nude, with her signature on one corner. His crotch clenches. Then he lifts up the silicon sex toy in the shape of a woman's bum with a pink orifice resembling a girl-part. He unfolds an instruction booklet, but it's in Japanese language so he tosses it away. Standing up, he unbuckles his belt and drops his pants. He returns to a sitting position on the edge of his bed, brings the fake bum to his groin and penetrates the orifice. Then he closes his eyes to imagine Suzuka Sakura straddling him and fumbles for the switch at the side of the toy.

He presses the switch, expecting a pleasurable sensation. "Aaaaaaarrrgh!" Eyes bugging wide, Dung screams in pain as an electric shock jolts through his dickie! He yanks the masturbator away, his face twisted in a grimace. *Shit! This product's faulty! Something's wrong with the wiring! Bloody cheap imitation products!*

"So, that's the story of Dung and Thuc," says Mr Kieu Nam, the apothecary, sitting across me in a coffee shop.

I take a sip of my tea. "How did you know this story?"

"The victim, Dung, came to my store to buy medicine for his man-part which was swollen." Mr Kieu Nam strokes his moustache. "He explained to me the cause of the swelling, and I sold him a bottle of bear gallbladder oil. I told him to rub the oil on his man-part twice a day." He lifts his porcelain cup and takes a sip. "Put this story in your book."

Phuket: Moon, Sand and Sex

Seated at a table with my feet buried in sugary sands up to the ankles, I flick my gaze up to the sky freckled with glittery stars. A full moon is glowing. All around me, party animals – pot-bellied men, muscular hunks, hot babes and not-so-hot girls-next-door – are dancing like string puppets. I focus on the four sexy dancers on the stage, about thirty feet away. They are gyrating, advancing, retreating, their limbs in constant motion and their bodies twisting in a seductive allure. Music from speakers is thumping so loud, I can almost feel my bones vibrating!

I am in Thailand's Phuket Full Moon Party at Paradise Beach, a golden sandy crescent drenched in moonlight, neon lights LED uplights and bistro lighting. I recall reading somewhere that small animals are more active during the full moon. And, believe it or not, a bouncer in Bangkok once remarked to me that, after fifteen years in the job, he knows that during full-moon nights, he can expect more fights in his nightclub as compared to other moonless nights. So, a full moon is ideal for a high-energy party.

The dancing on the stage stops and a fire show begins on the beach, but people are blocking my view and I only hear drumming. I rise from my chair and jostle to the front. Four muscular bare-chested men are twirling poles with both ends burning, creating circles of fire. Next, they pass the poles from their right hands to their left hands backwards. Legs stamping, they execute this move several times. The crowd cheers! Now they pass the burning poles from front to back repeatedly under their legs! Great balls of fire! The crowd roars! The fire show ends with a handsome hunk swinging a poi in circles and geometric patterns, their blazing trials sending sparks into the cool air.

Some fella on the stage shouts into a mike, "It's limbo time!" Island music fills the air, its syncopated rhythm setting my sandaled foot tapping the sands.

Two fire dancers set up a burning stick about four or five feet long between two notched wooden stands. They take the lead by bending backwards and going under the waist-high stick.

"All dancers, please line up behind the stick!"

More than a dozen men and women form a line about ten feet away from the stick and, one by one, they limbo under the flaming stick safely. The two fire dancers lower the stick one notch. A daredevil babe in a tank top and jeans shorts passes the stick. Up next is a fat man who has a mop of hair resembling tumbleweed. He staggers on unsteady thick legs under the flaming stick, his belly protruding forward, his belly-button exposed under the hem of his t-shirt.

"Go! Go! Go!" yells the crowd.

A man shrieks, "My God! His hair has caught fire!"

"Eeeeeeek!" screams a woman standing beside me.

A young first-aider, identified by his t-shirt and first-aid box in hand, rushes towards the fatso. The first-aider does a double-take as the butterball yanks off his wig and tosses it to the ground. He is as bald as an egg! Casting a lingering glance at the smouldering wig, he laughs off the incident and disappears into the crowd.

Aw, all's well that ends well.

The party continues with fireworks bursting in flares of vermillion, green and blue like fiery blooms, their sudden bangs almost making me shudder. Alas, the event ends with the burning of the Phuket Full Moon Party sign, strung between two coconut trees. What a fun-filled night. I'll be back again.

* * *

I am sauntering down Patong's Bangla Road which is packed with ATMs, tour agencies and establishments offering booze, women, music and massage. Garish neon lights shimmering, sparkling and flashing illuminate a motley collection of characters – touts, bouncers, hookers, leaflet-toting promotional girls and street vendors donned in glow-in-the-dark hairbands – lurking on the sidewalk on both sides. Loud thumping music blasting from disco, bars and nightclubs can wake the dead.

At Soi Sea Dragon, I head to Suzy Wong's Go-Go Bar, which has a reputation for its drop-dead gorgeous girls. A pair of stone lions atop pedestals guard its Chinese-styled wooden doors fitted with bronze ring knockers. Two sex kittens holding foam tubes spank me on the bum – there's a loud squeak but it's painless – as they push open the doors to a hidden paradise and usher me in. Inside, my butt sinks down on a leather chaise backed by red drapes with a valance. I order a beer which comes with my bill. No unpleasant surprises here. Curvy dancers clad in G-strings and cropped Chinese-style camisoles – all beautiful enough to grace the front covers of men's magazines – are gyrating on a stage and, suddenly, two balding *farangs* step up to spank their butts with foam tubes. Three hotties creep behind the *farangs* and start whacking their bums, amidst giggles.

The ass-spanking scene reminds me of what Dr. Dulcinea Pitagora, a Manhattan-based certified sex therapist and psychotherapist, said in her web talk show titled Kink Doctor,

"Spanking can enhance excitement and physical sensations; increase adrenalin, endorphins, and oxytocin; explore and maybe push the line between pleasure and pain; increase intimacy and bonding."

I decide that before my excitement shoots up to an uncontrollable level, I should finish my beer quickly and leave. Next, I totter to Devil's Playground – also owned by the Suzy Wong Group – further down the road.

Guarded by two lasses dressed in red and wearing hairbands with red blinking horns, Devil's Playground sports a mock cave entrance. Stepping inside, I enter a massive ovoid space with a stage in the centre. With faux rock walls and a rock ceiling around me, I feel like I'm cocooned in the earth's body. The patrons are focusing their bulging eyes on the four bikini-clad go-go dancers wearing red horns and gyrating on a small stage. The music is hot and the she-devils are even hotter. All are sporting elastic ties wrapped in a crisscross pattern on one leg each.

I plop down on a banquette with small round tables stationed at equal intervals, grab a beer and watch the dancing. Sweet thunderation! The performance is a display of quivering butt cheeks and bouncing gazongas. Heat invades my loins. I gulp. Shall I sell my soul to the Devil? The music stops. But only for a moment. The four she-devils leap off the stage and four lasses garbed in skimpy white luminous costumes and knee-high stockings replace them. They also wear little wings behind their backs. They're angels! Hallelujah! I am baptized and saved by them! Temptation banished to Hell, I finish my beer, take my leave to continue my nocturnal exploration.

I backtrack out of Soi Sea Dragon, continue down Bangla Road and dive into an alley across. A stout woman, mid-thirties, and sporting a bob hairdo is standing on the sidewalk outside a massage shop. She hollers at me as I pass by, "Masaaaaage! Masaaaaage! Masaaaaage!" Smiling, she strides forward to block my path and offers me a leaflet but I cross my arms across my chest. "You can have a sandwich massage!" she says, holding a leaflet in my face.

I flick my gaze from the prices on the leaflet to her bad-ass face. "What's a sandwich massage?"

"You are sandwiched between two girls! Both naked! Oooooh! Very nice!"

"I'm not interested, thank you." I sidestep her.

"Why?" Her friendliness evaporates like rain on a desert. "You don't like girls?" "Then you go for ladyboy massage!" she sneers, pointing down an alley further ahead. "There, there's one down the road!"

I continue my stroll on Bangla Road and, after passing more go-go bars and discos, I turn down another alley. A sign "Yoni Massage" outside a shop grabs my attention. I step up to a scrawny late-forties woman loitering outside and stop a few feet away from her. "What's yoni massage?"

"Massage the girl-parts."

My jaw goes slack. "Huh? Is this for lesbians?"

"Not necessarily. Yoni massage also benefits straight woman. Our massage therapist will work on the head, shoulders, body and, finally, the girl-parts. The massage releases blocked negative energy, allowing the woman to enjoy sex better. Some clients achieve orgasm and squirt."

"What! Happy ending for women?"

"Why don't you bring your girlfriend or wife here? Our massage therapist will turn her into a cock-hungry woman! Then you can fuck her more often!" She chuckles, revealing a gap between her big middle teeth.

Eeeeek! I gape at her crass language, heat braising my cheeks from embarrassment, and fish out a handkerchief to wipe off the sudden beads of sweat in my brows. "I'm gay," I lie, "I don't have a girlfriend or wife."

***

Walking down a neon-choked alley, twenty-something Frankie Fraser (not his real name) of Christchurch, New Zealand, gawks at the female promoters standing outside bars and discos. On his first flush trip to Thailand, he is eager to seek new exciting experiences.

A young tout with tattoos on his neck grabs Frankie by the wrist and stops him from walking. "Ping pong show, sir," says the tout. "Buy one beer and watch the show free!" He hands over a menu to Frankie who reads it.

On the menu is written:

Pussy sexy dance, Pussy shoot balloon, Pussy open bottle, Pussy smoke cigarette, Pussy blow candle, Pussy cut banana, Pussy write love letter, Pussy swallow razor blades, Pussy eat fish, Pussy drink Coca-Cola, Lesbian show, Man & woman fucking show.

A devilish glimmer shine from Frankie's eyes. "How much is the beer?" Excitement throbs in his voice.

"One hundred baht only."

Wariness creeps into Frankie's veins. "Are you sure?"

"Yes, I'm sure." The tout's voice is low, smooth and disarming. "Sir, if it's not one hundred baht, you can just leave and walk off safely, I swear to Lord Buddha."

"Where's the place?"

The tout takes back the menu, turns on his heels and walks down the alley. "Please follow me, sir."

Further ahead, Frankie follows the tout up a staircase where a toad-faced bouncer with a barrel chest and a penitentiary haircut is seated at a scuffed wooden desk at the entrance to a hall.

"Please hand over your mobile phone, sir," says the toad-faced bouncer to Frankie. "We don't allow any secret recording of the show." He takes out a piece of paper and a pen and puts them on top of the desk. "Please write your first name or any initials," he grunts. "It's to identify your mobile phone."

Frankie scrawls his first name on the paper and hands over his Moby. The toad-faced bouncer ties the paper to the phone with a rubber band and drops it into an open drawer at his side. "Don't forget to collect your phone after the show."

Frankie nods and casts a glance over his shoulder. The tout is gone. A tanned shoulder-length-haired waitress – probably late twenties and having a bulbous nose – ushers Frankie to a small table facing a stage with a glittery curtain. Several other tables are also taken up by patrons, mostly men. The waitress goes away.

A minute later, she returns and places a froth-topped stein of beer and a bill on the table. "Payment now, please."

Frankie stares wide-eyed at the bottom figure. Sweet thunderation! The bill is 1300 baht or about USD42. "Come on, your tout says it's only one hundred baht."

"What tout? We don't employ touts."

"Sorry, I'm leaving." Frankie gets up from his metal chair.

An enormous bouncer with a Mohican haircut appears out of the woodwork, clamps a gnarled hand on Frankie's shoulder and pushes him down. "Sit down, mister! The show's going to start! You cannot leave until the show is over."

Goose flesh rippling up his back, Frankie plops back on the metal chair and takes out two money notes from his wallet. "Here, one thousand five hundred baht."

"Thank you, sir." A smile tugs at the waitress' hard-looking lips. "I'll keep your change as tip." Wearing a smug expression, she struts away on kitten heels.

Frankie's jaw drops. The bouncer goes away. The show begins five minutes later.

* * *

Standing in the foyer of the arrival lounge in Phuket International Airport, Samorn, aged twenty-six, scans the blur of people on a KLM flight from Cardiff coming out of the exit gates. Wearing jeans, she has a short, slim frame and shiny black hair flows from a centre part to her shoulders. Her oval face is devoid of make-up.

A melee of faces surges forward like a river current flowing to their destinations, with small groups of people stopping to cause an eddy. Thirty-year-old Reuben Collier (not his real name) – a fabricator welder of Aberystwyth, Wales – dressed in a pair of sports cargo pants and a t-shirt, pushes his way through the crowd towards Samorn. They wrap their arms around each other for several moments and disengage to look into each other's eyes.

Reuben's dark brown eyes twinkle with anticipation. "Darling, have you told your parents?" He has a long face and a nose that looks like it has been broken a few times.

"They're eager to meet you, dear." Samorn holds Reuben's hand and leads him out of the airport to the parking lot, their shadows thrown short by the late morning sun. "I've bought tickets for the Phuket Smart Bus. The journey will be interesting for you as it stops at all the beaches on the west coast. From Bangtao Beach to Surin Beach, Kamala, Patong Beach, Karon, Kata Beach and finally Rawai."

Two hours later, the bus stops at Rawai Beach near a long pier and the couple alight along with other passengers, mostly tourists.

"Let's go to the Sea Gypsy Fish Market first." Samorn points down the tree-lined road. "We'll buy some seafood back for my *Mae* to cook. Seafood here is cheap."

Samorn, her *Phx*, *Mae*, older sister Apinya and Reuben are sitting at a round wooden table which is crammed with bowls of sour-prawn soup and platters of turmeric fried trevally, tamarind steamed snapper and basil squid. The five people are ensconced in the small dining room of a wooden home in Rawai village and a squeaky fan is pirouetting above their heads.

Samorn's *Phx*, probably mid-fifties, flicks his gaze from his plate of rice to Reuben and rambles something in Thai language before jabbing a piece of squid and popping it into his mouth. He looks at Apinya through sunken eyes, nods and starts to chew his food.

Apinya interprets what her *Phx* said, "My father said his father was a sea gypsy who worked as a pearl diver. Every day, Grandpa dived to the bottom of the ocean without goggles or scuba equipment to search for oysters. He also collected sea urchins, clams and seaweed. His work caused him to become deaf eventually because of pressure from sea water on the eardrums. That's why my *Phx* didn't want to follow his footsteps and became a motorcycle mechanic instead."

Samorn lifts her glass of tea and gulps a mouthful. "I've one-quarter sea gypsy blood in me." She wipes her bee-stung lips with a piece of tissue paper.

"How interesting." Reuben takes a slurp of the sour-prawn soup from a small bowl at his side. "Then you've a diver's genes in you and can swim like a fish."

Samorn and Apinya chortle.

Phx says something again and Apinya interprets, "Let's get to the purpose of your visit. I understand you want to marry Samorn. By now, you should now that *sinsod* is a part of Thai culture. So how much *sinsod* are we looking at?"

Reuben puts down his fork and spoon. "Sixty thousand baht." He sits straighter. "I can also budget for a traditional wedding here."

"*Hk Hmun bath*," Samorn says to her *Phx*. "*Chan samarth tha ngbpraman sahrab ngan taegngan baeb dangdeim dithi ni.*"

Phx casts a sideway glance at his fat wife who says something, and he considers for a moment before uttering a reply.

Pinya asks, "Can you buy a matrimonial home for my daughter?"

Reuben feels a lump in his throat. "Err, not at the moment, I need some time to sort out my finances." *Gee, I need to sell my car and flat first.*

Samorn says to *Phx*, "*Chan txngkar wela ni kar cadkar dan karngein khxng chan.*"

Phx continues through Pinya, "I've a small piece of land, not beachfront but on the eastern fringe of the village. I'll be happy to give it to both of you as a gift. However, foreigners cannot own land in Thailand, so I'll transfer it to Samorn and both of you can build a house on the property. Can you bear the construction cost of the house?"

"If it's by progressive payments for a small house, yes." *With overtime work, I should be able to do it.*

Smiling, Samorn puts down her fork and spoon. "Oh, darling, isn't that wonderful?" She claps her dainty hands, her thick lips upturned at the corners.

"Can we go see the land?"

"Sure, it's sandwiched between two single-storey houses, about three thousand over square feet, but is now covered with undergrowth. Tomorrow, we can take a tuk-tuk to pass the land and I'll point it out to you."

Phx speaks and Apinya interprets, "When the house is completed, both of you can get registered. Then you can move to Phuket to start your welding business. In the meantime, why don't both of you get engaged?"

Reuben's face glows with joy. "That's a great suggestion!"

Aberystwyth, Wales

Sitting in his bedroom, Reuben activates Skype on his laptop and moments later, Samorn appears on the screen. The rows of computers behind her show that she in a cybercafé.

"Darling, my *Phx* used his savings to begin the construction of our house. Please check your Gmail." Samorn tucks a few strands of stray hair behind her ears, her emerald engagement ring glinting from light of the PC screen. "I've sent you a link to a video in Google Drive. The video shows the work-in-progress of our house."

"This is a surprise." Reuben rubs his chin. "What's the hurry?"

"Why delay our marriage, dear?" Samorn takes out a piece of paper with Thai scripts and holds it to the webcam for a second. "This is the title deed, the land has been transferred to me, darling. Can you wire some money to me? I want to repay my *Phx*, don't want to be indebted to him. I've also attached a layout plan of our house in my email – I drew it myself."

"Sure, let me check the video." Reuben squishes his eyebrows. "Can I make minor amendments in the layout?"

"Sure, but be quick about it."

Five minutes later, Reuben watches the video that Samorn sent to him. In the opening shot of the mobile phone video, she is standing inside a work site fenced on four sides by rusty zinc sheets. Then the scene shows two hatted workers digging trenches to prepare the foundation of the house. Next, Samorn is walking along the length of one trench. She stops to talk briefly to one worker and the video camera closes the distance to her half-figure, and she shows a thumbs-up. End of the three-minute video.

Another month passes ...

Looking at the screen of his laptop. Reuben says into the built-in mike, "Darling, I've wired more money to you last week. How's the construction of our house progressing?"

"Fine, they're doing the framing now." Samorn clears her throat. "I've resigned from the go-go bar, dear. Now, I'm a cashier in Quik Mart, Thawiwong Road, just beside the post office."

"I'm happy you're out of the bar industry for good. I'll be flying to Phuket in a fortnight's time. I'll email you my flight details."

"I may or may not be able meet you at the airport, depending on my shift." Samorn puckers her lips in a kiss. "I love you, darling. Bye."

A fortnight later ...

Sitting in the back of a tuk-tuk, Reuben is heading to Samorn's piece of land in Rawai village which he visited with her more than three months ago. His lips are gummed in a straight line and his eyes are glossy from concern.

Three hours ago, after having arrived in Phuket International Airport, he called Samorn but she did not answer his call. Then he took a *tuk-tuk* to Quik Mart in Patong but Samorn was not there. The staff said they never heard of her. He then went to her former go-go bar and the bartender said she has resigned.

The *tuk-tuk* stops at a spot beside the road. "We've arrived, sir," says the driver.

Reuben sticks his head out of the side of the *tuk-tuk* and looks across the road. The land, sandwiched between two old houses, is covered in undergrowth.

Huh? Reuben's eyebrows shoot upward and his eyes expand wider in shock. It's still the same as before! *WTF! The video was shot elsewhere! I've been scammed! I bet the land doesn't even belong to her or her old man.*

* * *

A year ago ...

Inside the hall of Roaring Bikers Bar (name changed), laughter from patrons and their hostesses is overpowering the jazz music. The hotties are garbed in body-hugging black t-shirts printed with white skulls, faded jeans shorts, faux leather boots and gloves. Even the ageing bartender has a bandana wrapped around his head and an old Harley Davidson Sportster is parked in one corner.

Mummy Pensri – her face like a brown withered apple – strides in knee-high boots to a table occupied by Siriporn and a fat foreigner with blond hair and a beard. "Your bill, sir." She puts the metal platter on the table. The fatso passes his credit card to Mummy who returns to the cashier's counter. A minute later, she takes long strides back to the butterball. "Sir, your credit card has been rejected. Can you pay cash, please?"

The roly-poly pulls out his wallet, opens it and looks inside. "Oh my God, I haven't brought enough cash with me." He jolts erect in his chair and spreads his hands. "Can I come back tomorrow with the money?"

"Don't take me as a sucker! You could be on the first flight out of Phuket tomorrow. You're a bloody free loader!" Mummy Pensri parks her hands on her hips and ponders for a second. "Instead of my bouncers roughing you up, I'll give you an alternative because I love challenges."

"Oh, how?"

"Let's play the knife game! If you win, I'll waive the bill. If you lose, you will clean up the bar after it closes – wash the toilets, mop the floor, empty the ashtrays, do everything."

"Sounds fair."

"Siriporn, get a knife from the kitchen."

Siriporn rises from her seat beside the fatso and clomps away in ankle-high boots.

Mummy Pensri pulls out a stool and sits across the wooden table facing the *farang*. She pulls the glove out of one hand, tosses it away and spreads her fingers. Siriporn returns and hands a five-inch carving knife with a pointed tip to Mummy. Its edge and tip glint menacingly under the overhead lights.

"Who has the higher number of stabs in thirty seconds wins." Mummy Pensri's eyes, squinty but sharp, moves from the butterball to Siriporn. "Siriporn, please time us."

Siriporn looks at her wrist watch. "Ready? Now!"

Mummy stabs the table from behind the thumb to the space between thumb and forefinger, moves forth to the next spaces and back again, simultaneously counting, "One! Two! Three! Four! Five! Six! Seven!..."

Siriporn delivers a karate chop in mid-air. "Stop!"

"Thirty-five!" Mummy releases an exhale. "Your turn!"

The fatso spreads one pudgy hand on the table, fixes his gaze on the former and repeats what Mummy has done, his lips steeled into a slit.

"Stop!"

"Thirty-five!" the roly-poly yells. "It's a tie! Hooray!"

"Let's go for round two. We'll do it blind folded this time." Mummy Pensri squares her shoulders. "Siriporn, please blindfold me with your scarf."

Siriporn steps behind Mummy Pensri, takes off her neck scarf and blindfolds the latter.

In thirty seconds, Mummy Pensri again manages thirty-five stabs. Next, Siriporn ties her scarf over the *farang*'s eyes.

"Go!" she hollers, mouth parting to reveal nicotine-stained teeth.

Tat-tat-tat-tat-tat-tat-tat-tat! The knife moves in a flurry for several seconds before it lands on the fatso's hand, blood spurting out of the wound.

"Arrrrgh!" yells the *farang* in pain, dropping the knife on the table.

Back to the present ...

"Baloney!" My lips up-turn into a half-smile. "Don't expect me to believe that story." I lean backward in my chair and scrunch my eyebrows.

"You don't believe my story?" Mummy Pensri removes the glove of her left hand. "Look! Look carefully! You see any scars? No scars because I always won at the knife game." She shoots a searing gaze at me. "You're think my story is fake? Never mind, but I challenge you to a knife game! Because I want to show you my skill. If you lose, you buy drinks for my girls! If you win, I'll waive your bill." She hollers at one of three girls at a nearby table. "Ratana, borrow a knife from our cook."

It's Happy Hours in Roaring Bikers Bar and I am the sole customer. Several bargirls are lounging in separate groups at tables, either fiddling with their mobile phones, or chatting with each other.

"You sure about this knife game, Mummy?"

"Of course!" Mummy snaps her head up. "You're not scared, are you?"

Togged up in a biker's outfit, Ratana returns from the kitchen and hands over a knife to Mummy Pensri.

"Thanks, ask Chakan to tap the tom-tom drum." Mummy Pensri raises two knobbly fingers. "Two taps per second!" She returns her attention to me and her eyes thin along with the press of her lips. "We'll stab according to the tempo of the drumming."

What! My heart beats faster. Gee ... I've never played the knife game before. "Err, there's no need for the knife game. I believe your story, Mummy." My chest tightens. "I'll buy drinks for your girls." I raise one hand. "Hey, bartender! Lady's drinks for Mummy's girls."

Mummy Pensri laughs. "Gotcha!"

"What's so funny?

Mummy tugs the glove out of her right hand, turns its upper side to face me. "What do you see?" She drops the glove on her lap.

My eyes jolt wider in shock. "Huh? What happened to your right hand?" Several klenoid scars are scattered on the top of her right hand and fingers. "Why are there so many injuries?"

"I've played the knife game several times before and mostly lost!" The seed of a smile sprouts on Mummy Pensri's face. "I'm left-handed!" Her smile glides into a smirk.

"Yay!" Ratana yells. "Mummy's a smart woman."

***

Christmas season ...
Thick lips upturned in a grin, Mummy Anong asks, "Do you know why a Christmas tree is better than a man?" She is lounging on a tub chair across from me in Happy Ending Bar (not its real name) on Rat-U-Thit Road.

Sitting beside me, twenty-something Phaelyn says: "Because it's always erect!" She's wearing a strap Santarina costume with a plunging neckline and the scent of jasmine wafting from her perfume feathers my nostrils.

I release a chuckle. "Well said!" I pick an olive from a platter of preserved tidbits and pop it into my mouth.

"Why is a priest like a Christmas tree?" Mummy Anong asks

again.

"Beats me!" I swing my gaze to Phaelyn and jut my chin. "You know the answer?"

Mummy Anong steps up to a Christmas tree a few feet away and palms a silvery ball. "Their balls are only for decoration!"

I chortle with the olive rolling on my tongue. The little rascal slides into the back of my throat and I choke. "Hack! Hack! Hack! Hack! Hack!" I bend forward and slap my chest repeatedly. I can't speak or cough as blood rushes to my face.

"Goodness, he's choking!" Phaelyn shrieks.

"I'll perform the Heimlich Manoeuvre on him!" Mummy Anong rushes back to our table. "Stand up, quick!"

I get to my feet and Mummy Anong steps behind me. She puts a clenched fist beneath my rib cage and grabs it with her other hand. Grunting like a raging bull, she pulls the clenched fist upward and backward several times. I feel like a gigantic python has coiled around me!

Phut! The olive flies out of my mouth. It hits the glass top of the steel bar table and ricochets into Phaelyn's cleavage!

"Eeeeeeek!" Phaelyn squeals. "A lecherous olive."

Phuket: Kisses in Breezes

I find a space between two blokes perched on stools, lean against the bar counter and catch the young bartender's eyes. The fella detaches himself from conversation with another patron and strolls over to me.

"Yes, sir?" he asks.

"Gimme a drink that is popular with gays."

The bartender waves a limp wrist. "One Vodka Red Bull coming up!"

I am inside Peter Pan Bar (not its real name) in Paradise Complex, Patong's one-stop centre for drag shows, go-go boys and men-only massage shops in Thailand. Sexy saxophone notes are dancing above the jangle of voices and cigarette smoke is spiralling in the air.

The bartender sidles away, returns and places a highball glass in front of me.

I take a sip of my cocktail through a straw and a hand pats me on the shoulder. I turn sideways to see that the owner of the hand is a handsome Thai man. His face consists of rugged angles broken by high cheekbones and a mane of dark hair curls from his forehead to just below his ears.

"Hello, darling," asks the man, "are you a burger?"

My eyebrows shoot up in surprise. "What do you mean?"

"Because you can be the meat between my buns!"

I chuckle at his pickup line and take a swallow. "Why don't you tell me your life story instead? I'll pay you a big tip." I gesture to an empty table nearby. "Let's go sit there." I extend my hand and he pumps it. "I'm Jackson," I lie.

"Darling, please call me Prayut." Prayut hollers at the bartender. "Gin and tonic."

Fifteen years ago ...

Carrying a small package wrapped in gift paper, Chaiyo, aged thirty-five, strides along the corridor and stops at an apartment. He jabs at the doorbell which chimes and he puts his right hand behind to hide the package. The door swings open to reveal Nattapong, aged twenty-eight, standing in the doorway. "How's your day at the office, *thirak* [darling]?" Nattapong asks, lips upturned in a smile. He is clad in faded denim jeans and a sleeveless t-shirt. His forehead is high and proud while Chaiyo has sharp and angled cheeks. But both men are handsome.

"Can be better, dear." Chaiyo steps inside the door foyer, bends to slip off his sneakers. "Had a tough presentation, boss shot tough questions at me." He waits until Nattapong has locked the door and turns around. "Surprise, darling!" He hands the small package to Nattapong.

"Oh, you shouldn't have, *thirak*." Nattapong takes the package and starts to walk to the bedroom. "Thank you so much." He casts a glance behind his shoulder at Chaiyo. "You want a beer?"

"Maybe later."

Nattapong and Chaiyo enter the bedroom, and the latter closes the door. They sit on the edge of the bed and Nattapong tears away the wrapping, revealing a cologne box. Nattapong's eyes shine with a twinkle. "Wow! It's an expensive brand!" He opens the box, takes out a bottle and splashes some cologne on

his neck. "Ooh, I like the woody fragrance – you know my taste."
He dabs a spot on his fingers and applies it behind Chaiyo's ear.
"Sharing is caring, *thirak*!" He repeats the process on his lover's
other ear and puts the bottle aside.

Nattapong and Chaiyo turn sideways to look into each other's
eyes, then they embrace and lock lips, their breathing becoming
faster. Soon, they strip and clatter the bed headboard against the
wall, their bodies joined as one.

Phutson picks up a rattan laundry basket and enters the bedroom.
Aged thirty, she wears short puffy waves of hair framing both
sides her face like a poodle's ears and is of average height. From
her dresser chair, she picks up a pair of panties and a brassier and
tosses them inside the basket. She strides across the bedroom to
a wall and yanks Chaiyo's shirt off a hook. Her nostril catches a
waft of fragrance. *Huh? Perfume?* She brings the shirt to her nose
and takes an inhale. *Odd smell. It's not my perfume.* Heat swarms
her cheeks. She ponders for several seconds and resumes her task
of collecting soiled clothes.

Togged up in a blouse and skirt, Phutson enters a perfume store in
Phuket Town with a paper bag and goes to the counter. She casts
a glance at her wrist watch. *I hope this won't take long. Prayut
would be out from school soon.* Phutson sits on a cushioned chair,
pulls the hem of her skirt down and puts the paper bag on her lap.

"Can I help you, Miss?" asks a young woman, togged up in
a smart uniform.

Phutson takes out a folded shirt. "Can you find out what the
perfume is on this shirt? I'd like to buy a bottle." *His birthday's
coming! I'd love to see the shock on his face when I give the*

perfume his girlfriend wears to him! She hands the shirt over to the sales assistant. *It'll give him a hint that I know that he's been cheating on me.*

The sales assistant takes the shirt, brings it to her nose and takes a sniff. She takes out a few bottles from a glass cupboard behind her and tests each bottle using paper strips. Finally, she puts a bottle of cologne in front of Phutson. "Madam, the fragrance from the shirt is from a men's cologne, not a woman's perfume. This is the bottle. You want to buy this?"

"Oh? I see." *Strange. Chaiyo hasn't used cologne before.* Phutson replaces the shirt in the paper bag. *Looks like he's wearing cologne discreetly.* "Sure, I'll take a bottle. Can you gift wrap it for me, please?" *I bet he has a bottle stashed away in his office room or car glove compartment.*

A fortnight later ...

Chaiyo picks up a toast and spreads butter on it. "Prayut, when's your final exams?" He replaces the butter knife back on its former spot on the table. He is wearing a sky-blue shirt that fits him like a glove and a necktie loosely knotted around an open-collar.

Seated across the table, twelve-year-old Prayut scoops a spoonful of chicken gruel into his mouth. "Next month."

"Have you started on your revision?"

"Yes, *Phx*." Prayut shifts in his seat. "I'm concentrating on my weaker subjects."

"More coffee, darling?" Phutson lifts up a coffee pot.

"Sure." Chaiyo rises and tosses a gaze at his son. "Prayut, finish your food quickly. When I'm back from the loo, we leave." Jamming the knot of his necktie against his Adam's apple, he strides to the bathroom next to the kitchen.

Phutson leans across the table, pours more coffee into Chaiyo's cup and drops two sugar cubes into it. Chaiyo's mobile phone lying on the spot where he was sitting rings. Phutson stretches an arm to pick it up and looks at the caller ID. *Natt. Short for either Nattaporn or Nattapong.* She jabs the answer button.

A Thai man's voice says, "Happy birthday, darling!"

Is this a man? Or a woman imitating a man's voice? Phutson's breath catches. *Maybe a ladyboy?* "Hello, who's this?"

"Oh, sorry, I got the wrong number!"

Click! The caller hangs up.

Is Chaiyo's lover a ladyboy? Phutson replaces the mobile phone on the table. *Let's see what happens tonight.*

Chaiyo pulls over the side of the road outside Wattana High School (not its real name) and Prayut gets out of the car, lugging his school bag. Chaiyo pulls into traffic and his handphone mounted on the dashboard chimes, its caller ID showing "Natt". He taps a button to go on speaker mode.

"Darling, I made a blunder!" Nattapong's voice is edgy.

"What blunder?"

"Your wife didn't tell you?"

Chaiyo casts a glance at the rear-view mirror. "No."

"Earlier, I called to wish you happy birthday and your wife answered the call!"

"Shit! You shouldn't call me unnecessarily!" Chaiyo toots his horn. "Please call me only when I'm at work on weekdays, okay?" He releases an exhale. "Weekends are family days for me. Bye, dear." *I better memorize his number and delete it.*

Hair spiked from a shower, Chaiyo comes out of the bathroom

in his sun-downer clothes and smelling of soap. An hour ago, he took dinner with his wife and son and the former didn't mention this morning's phone call. He saunters to the living room, sits in front of the TV and switches it on using the remote control. From the kitchen out walks Prayut with a birthday cake in both hands, accompanied by Phutson, wearing an apron. "Happy birthday, *Phx*!" Prayut puts the cake on the coffee table.

Chaiyo jerks upright. *I was expecting this*. "Thank you, son."

Phutson and Prayut sing "Happy Birthday" and Chaiyo blows out the sole candle.

From the front pocket of her apron, Phutson takes out a small package. "Happy birthday, darling!"

"You're so wonderful!" Chaiyo unwraps the package and his eyes bulge. *Shit! It's the same cologne I gave to Nattapong! She's trying to tell me something*. "I haven't worn cologne before. You want me to start, dear? Want me to smell nice – that's thoughtful of you!" A lump forms in his throat.

Phutson releases a mirthless chuckle. "Marinate in it to attract women or ladyboys." She smiles and juts her chin in the direction of the cake. "Come, cut the cake and let's eat."

The lump in Chaiyo's throat grows bigger. *I'm going to call Nattpong tomorrow, tell him we should stop seeing each other for a while till the heat is over*. Chaiyo shifts forward in his seat, lift a plastic knife and slices the cake into smaller pieces.

Three months later …

Chaiyo stirs from his sleep after hearing a short buzz on his mobile phone lying on the side table. He blinks a few times and turns his head sideways to the left. Clad in a baby doll nightgown, Phutson is lying beside him, her eyes closed. He turns his head to the right. The alarm clock shows 2:30 am. He props up on one elbow and looks at his mobile phone. *There's a missed call from Natt!* Chaiyo casts a wary glance at his wife again, grabs his mobile phone and steals out of the bed on tip-toe.

Inside the living room, he calls Nattapong. "Hello, dear, anything urgent?" His voice is a half-whisper.

"I'm outside your house, darling."

"What!" Chaiyo's jaw drops. "Are you mad? What're you doing here?"

"I couldn't sleep, darling – I miss you." Nattapong's tone of voice is pregnant with longing. "Can we meet for a while? Satisfy my yearning for you – give me your kisses and warm embrace."

A surge of liquid fire invades Chaiyo's loins. "Where are you?"

"Across the road, one house further down, in my car parked near the lamp post."

Chaiyo tip-toes to the front door. "Alright, I'll come out."

Lying on a pillow within a circle of lemon light cast by the side table lamp, Phutson opens her eyes. *He thought I didn't hear his phone ring, eh?* She gets down from the bed, strides across the bedroom and opens the door a crack. Light is coming from the living room. She slips out of the bedroom and goes to the kitchen. *He's not here.* After checking Prayut's room, she goes to the front door and notices that the key is missing from its hook on one wall. *He's gone somewhere and taken the key with him.* Phutson returns to the bedroom, takes her handbag from the dresser table and fishes out the spare key to the front door. She unlocks the front door and steps into the front porch.

She stands beside Chaiyo's car and looks to the left and right.

Her car is parked outside the front gate and, further ahead, a car is stationd under a lamp post. *That's not the neighbour's car. The windows are wound down, silhouettes of two people inside the front seats. If only I had a pair of binoculars!* She ponders for a tick. She returns to the bedroom and, from a drawer in the clothes closet, takes out a Canon EOS 200D camera belonging to Chaiyo. She goes to the front gate, aims the lens of the camera in a space between two grille bars and zooms to the maximum. *Oh Lord Buddha! Two men are petting and kissing!* She observes the smooching for about five minutes. Then the passenger-seat door opens and the interior overhead light automatically turns on, illuminating the two men. *I can't believe this! It's Chaiyo!* Still garbed in pyjamas, Chaiyo hops out of the car, presses the door shut and saunters to the front gate of his house. *My God! He's gay!* The camera drops to the cement floor with a thud. *My only escape from this nightmare is a divorce!*

A year later ...

Hunched over a textbook inside his bedroom, Prayut hears his mobile phone rings. He picks it up, sees an unknown number and taps the answer button. "Hello? Yes? I'm Prayut."

"Hello, son, it's me, *Phx*."

"Oh, it's you." Annoyance sears through Prayut like a high-voltage wire "What is it regarding, *Phx*?" He picks up a ballpoint pen.

"How are you? Doing okay in your studies?"

"Yes! Yes! Yes! I'm fine!" Prayut twirls the pen around his fingers. What do you want?" Exhaling aloud, he releases a hint of annoyance in his voice.

"I'm coming to Phuket in two days' time. Can we meet up?"

"What for?" A rash of heat crawls up Prayut's neck. "*Mae* loved you but you betrayed her, cheated her, hurt her! She cried to sleep many nights!"

"No matter what happened between me and your *Mae*, I still love you, son."

"You're a bloody womaniser, *Phx*!" Prayut turns sideways at the waist and throws the pen against the wall to assuage his hatred for his father. "Don't call me again! I hate you! I hate you! I hate you!" He ends the call.

Thirteen years pass ...

"Dinner's ready!" hollers Phutson, walking to the dining table cluttered with platters of food and setting a big bowl of *tom yum kung* in the centre. Prayut and a middle-aged man are seated at the table, talking in low voices, and a ceiling fan is spinning, swirling the citrusy aroma of lemongrass from the *tom yum kung* in the room.

From the hall, Mayuree, twenty-something, steps into the dining room with a handsome man, his hair neatly plastered down. "*Phx*, this is my boyfriend Anurak." She pulls out a chair for Anurak, its legs sliding against the polished marble floor. "That's my stepmother Phutson and my stepbrother Prayut."

Anurak clasps his hands and tilts his head in a slight bow. "*Sawade-kap*, Mr Theevarit, Mrs Phutson Theevarit, Prayut." He sits down with his back straight.

Phutson tosses a gaze at Prayut. "Son, I think it's time you bring a girlfriend home to show us."

Mr Theevarit chips in, "Yes, why are all your friends bachelors? I'm sure you've female co-workers? Some of them must be nice girls."

Prayut's throat constricts. "The only nice thing about my female colleagues is that their tattoos are spelled correctly!"

Everybody in the room chortles and the tightness in Prayut's throat dissipates.

A month passes ...

Hair slicked down with pomade, Prayut steps into Lusty Lads Club (not its real name), a gay bar in Patong. He is wearing cologne and a brown slim-cut short-sleeved shirt with button-down collars. With each beat of his heart, his gnarled ass throbs with desire as he has not been laid for several weeks. Tonight, he is seeking a sex partner. Prayut scans the room which has about a dozen tables and a small dance floor filled with gyrating same-sex couples. He goes to the bar and climbs up onto a tall bar stool. "Draught beer," he says to the bartender.

A stein topped with a layer of froth lands with a soft thud in front of Prayut. He picks up the stein, swivels around on the stool to face the other patrons. He takes a glug, his eyes searching for a man sitting alone. A handsome hunk lounging on a chair at the second-row table in the centre bolts upright and sails a slow gaze around the room. Prayut's eyes meet his. *Wow! He's so good-looking!* Prayut's asshole clenches! Wrapped in a tight short-sleeved t-shirt, the hunk smiles, cocks his head in the direction of the doorway and rises. He walks away and casts a glance over his shoulder at Prayut. Prayut lifts his stein, upends it and clunks it down on the counter.

Outside, the hunk walks a short distance, casting another back glance at Prayut, before turning into a dark side alley. Prayut follows him. The hunk is leaning sideways on his shoulder against a wall, beefy arms crossed over his broad chest. Prayut walks up to him, stops about two feet away and smiles. "Nice butt you have there. What time does it open?"

"A smile lures you away so easily, huh?" With a snarl, the hunk grabs Prayut's shirt front and pulls out a flash of steel from his trouser side pocket, the former's gaze hardening to ice. "You stupid faggot!" He holds the knife at Prayut's throat, his forearm bulging with muscles. "This is a stickup! Give me your wallet!"

Prayut's scrotum shrivels! He dips his hand into his jeans back pocket, plucks out his wallet and hands it over to the hunk. The hunk slips the wallet inside his side pocket. "I'll take that gold chain, too!" As the hunk reaches out to pull away the necklace, Prayut immobilises the former's knife hand by holding the wrist with both his hands. As quick as a pecking bird, he leans forward and bites the hunk's hand with all his might.

"Aaarrgh!" the hunk releases the knife, but he takes a step forward and knees Prayut in the groin.

"Ugh!" Prayut sinks to his knees, clutching his groin, his face distorted in a grimace.

The hunk holds both hands together, raises them above his head and hammers on the back of Prayut's head. Prayut falls flat on his face, squashing his nose, and blood trickles out. More blows and kicks land on him. The last thing he remembers is a circle of light becoming smaller and smaller until it disappears.

Phutson and Theevarit step inside the ward that Prayut has been admitted to and scan the two rows of beds, the smell of antiseptic clawing at their nostrils. Earlier, Phutson got a phone call from a policeman who got her number from Prayut's mobile phone.

The couple spot Prayut's bed easily by the presence of a young policeman talking with a grizzled doctor garbed in a white uniform. They take long strides to the policeman and the doctor goes away. Prayut is lying in bed unconscious, his head bandaged and his nose swollen to twice its normal size.

Phutson gasps in horror. "Oh, what happened?" She bends and strokes Prayut's face gently.

Theevarit steps up to the policeman and asks, "Officer, what happened to my stepson?"

The policeman takes off his peaked cap. "He was robbed and beaten unconscious, suffered a broken rib, too. Two passers-by found him lying on the ground in an alley." He tucks the cap under one arm.

Phutson joins her husband at his side. "Where?"

"Near a gay bar called Lusty Lads. According to witnesses, he was inside the bar, picked up a man but got robbed instead." The policeman clucks his tongue. "I'll be questioning the bartender tomorrow; maybe he can give a description of the guy he picked up."

Phutson and Theevarit look at each other, baffled but suspicious.

The next day ...

Phutson raps on the door of Prayut's bedroom, turns the knob and enters, squealing its hinges. Her son is lying in bed and reading a paperback, his bandaged head propped up on the headboard by two pillows. "Yes, *Mae*?" Prayut puts the book on the side table.

"Prayut," Phutson asks as she moves to sit at the end of the bed, "what were you doing in Lusty Lads Bar?"

"I went for a drink, *Mae*."

"But you know that Lusty Lads is a notorious gay bar, isn't it?" Phutson locks gazes with Prayut, draws in a heavy dose of air and releases it. "Tell me honestly, are you gay? Is that why you've no girlfriends?"

"Is it important, *Mae*?"

"Of course, it's important!" Phutson raises her voice a decibel, her eyes probing Prayut's with intensity. "I divorced your father because he's gay!"

"What!" Prayut jerks to a sitting position, his eyes doubling in size from shock. "But you told me he was fooling around with other women. I remember you labelled him as a 'serial womaniser'."

"I lied to you. I didn't want you to be ashamed of him, knowing that he's gay." Phutson shakes her head in despair. "But it looks like the last laugh is on me!" She sucks in a lungful of air as if it contains the courage to seek the truth. "Tell me honestly, Prayut – are you gay?"

"Y-yes, *Mae*."

"Oh Lord Buddha!" Prayut's answer slashes through Phutson with such anguish it sucks the air from her lungs, leaving her with a gasp. "How many tons of bad karma have I brought with me in this life?" She throws her arms up in sheer frustration, tears springing to her eyes. "Prayut, please get out of my life – our lives. Your stepfather and I are homophobic towards your kind. Your presence in our home may strain my relationship with my husband. And he has been a good husband to me."

"Can you tell me how to contact *Phx*?"

"I don't know. Why?"

A muscle jerks beneath the coffee-coloured skin of Prayut's throat. "I need to ask for forgiveness from him."

With nary a word, Phutson gets off the bed and strides out of the room.

Two years later ...

Prayut swerves his car into the parking lot of Pretty Parrot Club (not its real name) at Kamala Beach.

Seated in the front passenger seat, Kriasee reaches out one hand and squeezes Prayut's crotch. "Darling, my place or your place after the party?"

"On the beach!" Prayut flashes a side gaze at his lover. "Let's get adventurous!"

"Ooooh, how exciting! Don't drink too much darling, alcohol provokes desire but takes away the performance!"

Prayut and Kriasee get out of the car and walk with linked hands towards the entrance of the club. At one side of the entrance, a poster on a metal display stand announces "LGBT Party Tonight! Admission by Ticket Only!"

Inside the club, the scene is of smoke twisting in curls, standing drinkers at the bar, same-sex couples snuggled in booths, loud conversations, back slapping, giggling, laughing, kissing, willybechers, pint glasses, shot glasses, tinkle of glass on glass, bodies moshing on the dance floor and fast-tempo music tumbling about like a cascade.

Prayut and Kriasee grab a table. After having partaken several drinks, Prayut goes to the loo. At the entrance, a middle-aged man coming out, almost collides into him. Prayut and the middle-aged man stare at each other, surprise etched on their faces.

"Oh Lord Buddha, *Phx*, it's you!" Surprise jerks Prayut's head back. "Where were you all these years?"

"Son, I'm so happy to see you again!" Chaiyo's pensive aged-lined features reflect the surprise he feels as he stares at Prayut. "For the past decade. I was working in a resort on Phi Phi Island. I came back two years ago."

"I'm sorry, *Phx*! I really am!" Contrition glows in Prayut's face. "*Mae* lied to me that she divorced you because of you were philandering – she never said you're gay."

"What're you doing here? You're gay too?"

"Yes, I am, *Phx*!" Prayut's eyes brim with empathy and love. "Now I know your circumstances, I know that if I were in your shoes, I would have cheated on my spouse too. I've misjudged you, *Phx*, please forgive me."

* * *

I step inside Long John Silver Club (name changed) in Paradise Complex, stand in the foyer of the entranceway and scan my environs. Shiny black coffee tables and dark leather chairs cram the hall with a small stage at the far end. Several tables are occupied by pairs of men and soothing jazz piano music is oozing out from hidden speakers. A hunk – togged up in a crop top and faded denims – sitting alone at a table casts his gaze at me and smiles. His torso is cut into six bricks that tapers into a slim waist, and his square-jawed symmetrical face can entice a woman to whisper with lust.

I saunter to him and plop down on the chair across him. "Are you an ago-go boy?" I extend my hand and my lips quirk in a smile. "I'm Jackson."

The hunk pumps my hand. "I'm a man-whore!" Holy cow! His handshake is like an eagle's grip and his voice is a deep masculine baritone.

"Whoa!" My jaw almost goes slack. "I'll buy you a couple of man-whore drinks! And give you a tip worthy of a man-whore! You tell me everything about yourself, deal?

A masculine mouth twitches at one end into a wry grin. "Deal!"

The man-whore and I bump fists. "What's your name, man-whore?"

"I'm Udom, Udom Songthem, originally from Hatyai."

So begins the man-whore's story ...

Hat Yai, ten years ago ...

Pot-bellied Sirichai Songthem pulls out a stool from under the square dining table, plunks down and grabs a sheaf of papers held together by a binder clip in an acrylic tray. He opens the binder clip and looks at each paper, one by one. *Electricity bill, water bill, grocery store bill, internet bill, wife's mobile phone bill, my phone bill ... Hmmm, where's my calculator?* He tosses the papers on the dining table and rises from the stool. *Udom must have taken it again.* Sauntering across the dining room, he enters his sixteen-year-old son's bedroom to search for his calculator. He scans the top of a writing desk strewn with pens, a message pad, a penknife, balls of crumpled rough paper and a few books. His calculator is not there. He pulls out the left drawer. It's crammed with books. He yanks out the right drawer. His calculator is there with several CDs. He grabs a handful of the CDs and scrutinises their front jackets. *Oh Lord Buddha! These are gay CDs! Hell, my son's a gay! Hope it's not too late to change him.*

A week later ...

Sitting in the driver's seat, Sirichai manoeuvres his car into an angled parking slot at the road shoulder, yanks the handbrake up and switches off the headlights. "Here we are, son," he says to Udom, sitting beside him. "I know this freelancer quite well.

So, there's nothing to be scared of. It's time you start to like girls instead of boys." He kills the engine. "Come, let's go."

Sirichai and Udom get out of the car and the former leads his son to a metal grille door at the side of a shop house further down the drag, its entrance shuttered. Sirichai jabs a doorbell button and, moments later, the metal grille door automatically opens with a clack! Sirichai tramps up a flight of cement staircase with his son following behind. As Sirichai is nearing the last step, he sees a pair of bare feet and their ankles stationed at the left side of a bright rectangle.

"*Sawadee-kah*," says a woman's voice.

"Hello, Bussaba, how are you?" Sirichai now sees slender thighs peeking from under the hem of a red miniskirt, then broad hips which lead to a slim upper torso with a massive rack encased in a grey tank top. As he steps up to the staircase landing, he finally sees the woman's face. She is in her thirties and has a small, straight nose and a wide full mouth painted matte brown.

Sirichai and Udom enter the hall of the apartment, and Bussaba swings the wooden door shut and locks it. His father goes to sit on a rattan sofa chair at a coffee table and Udom joins him.

With a waddle of her big butt, the woman moves to sit across the duo and crosses her legs at the knees. "So, this is your son you spoke to me about on the phone?" She smiles, creating dimples on both cheeks. "He's as handsome as the father. What's his name?"

"Udom, sixteen years old." Sirichai pulls out his wallet and slips out some money notes. "This is payment in advance." He stretches one hand across the coffee table and passes the money to Bussaba.

"Ooooh! I like your style, *thirak*! That's why you're one of my favourite customers!" Bussaba slips the money notes in her cleavage. "Can I get you a drink?"

"No need, thanks." Sirichai casts a sideway glance at his son. "Udom, Bussaba will teach you to be a real man!" He chuckles and slaps his knees.

Bussaba rises. "Come, my boy, follow me to my bedroom." Her light steps take her to the end of the hall and to the doorway of her room.

Fifteen minutes pass. The door of Bussaba's bedroom swings open halfway and she hollers, "Sirichai, we've a problem."

Sirichai leaps up from his chair and, in a few quick bounds, moves to the doorway and steps inside the room. "What's the matter?"

Her hair tousled, Bussaba, wrapped in a bathing towel, points at Udom, lying naked in bed. "I've given him foreplay for more than ten minutes but he's like a dead fish!"

Sirichai closes the door and latches it. "Son, let me show you how it's done!" He drops his pants, steps out of them and pulls his boxers down to his ankles.

"Huh!" Udom springs to a sitting position. "*Phx*, I never knew you've such a small dick!"

Bussaba sniggers, her breasts quivering like jelly.

"Aw, fuck!" The embarrassment on Sirichai fuses into a miff and then blossoms into a reluctant grin. "At least I fathered you!"

Hatyai, two years ago ...

Kwanjai is lounging on an armchair and watching a soap opera on TV when she hears the front door behind her open and close. She switches off the TV using the remote control, rises and patters on bare feet to the dining room from the living hall. Akara Karnthip, her husband of two years, kicks off his sneakers, nudges them to one corner with his foot and saunters to the dining room with a sports bag in one hand.

This morning before leaving for work, thirty-year-old Akara, a production supervisor of a rubber glove factory, told Kwanjai that he would be home late as he would be going to the gym for his weekly workouts.

At the dining table, Kwanjai lifts up a pandanus-leaf woven food cover to reveal platters of *gaeng keow wan kai, pad phak* and *pak boong*. As she is scooping rice from a container on two plates, Akara goes to sit at the table. She flicks a glance from the plate in her hand to her husband and her eyes jolt wider. *Oh Lord Buddha, his shirt!* "*Thirak*, are you trying to build strength with your workouts? Or are you trying to look good naked?" She hands over a plate to Akara.

Akara puts the plateful of rice in front of him. "I want to keep fit and healthy." He spears a piece of chicken to his plate with a fork.

"What machines did you work out at?" Kwanjai shoots a glare at her husband. "How long at each machine? Did you go to any other place after your workout?"

"Huh? Why all these questions?"

"The fun of asking questions is finding out what a man does and contrast it with the lies he tells."

Akara gapes. "Huh? What do you mean?" Grains of rice drop from his mouth back to his plate. "Why're you staring at me like this?"

"Why're you wearing a different shirt? This morning, you put on a navy-blue shirt, now you're wearing sea blue."

Akara looks down at his shirt front and jerks upright in

shock. "Oh! I accidentally got soap in my eyes in the showers. In the lockers, I was squinting and I guess I took someone else's shirt by mistake."

A room furnished with a queen bed in Khwam Rak Inn (not its real name), Phetkasem Road, Hatyai, is in semi-darkness save for a halo of orange light cast by the bedside table lamp. From under a floral print blanket come groans and moans and the slurping sound of fellatio. Men's clothes are strewn all over the carpeted floor beside the bed.

The doorbell rings once. It rings again, longer and seemingly impatient and insistent.

Under the blanket, Akara and Udom untangle from each other's limbs. They stick their heads out of the blanket.

Wisps of hair hanging over his eyes, Akara props himself up on one elbow and lies on his side. "Shit! I wonder who's that?" He wipes saliva from the corner of his mouth with one hand.

Udom pushes aside the long hair fallen across his forehead from the top of his head "Maybe room service got the wrong room?"

A loud thumping is now coming from the front door.

Akara gets out of bed and pushes stray strands of hair from his eyes. "Could be an emergency in the hotel." He strides to a chair at the writing desk and flicks a bath towel off its back. "I better check who's at the door." He wraps the towel around his lower torso.

Udom sits up, draws his knees up and leans against the headboard. "Phew, I'm pooped from the sucking!" He draws in a big gulp of air and releases it.

As Akara is reaching for the door handle after turning the

lock, the doorbell rings again. He flings open the door. His jaw drops. "Oh Lord Buddha, it's you!"

Kwanjai and her burly brother – a bear of a man – barge into the bedroom.

She stares wide-eyed at the muscular naked man in bed and, then, at her husband and points a trembling finger at the latter. "My goodness! You're gay!" Anger turns to hurt. "W-why did you marry me in the first place?" Her voice is almost a choked sob.

Meanwhile, Udom leaps from the bed, grabs his pants lying in a pile on the floor beside the bed and jumps into them.

Kwanjai's brother glares at Udom. "You faggot! What's your name?"

Cringing, Udom picks up his briefs and sandals from the floor and bolts away barefooted from the room as if his feet were on fire.

"Tell me!" Kwanjai stamps one foot on the carpeted floor. "Why did you marry me?"

Kwanjai's brother shakes his head, leaves the room and closes the door behind him. He waits in the corridor.

"I thought I could be normal, lead a normal life and have a family, but the attraction was too strong." Akara's posture, normally erect and proud, curves like a sloppy macaroni. "C-can you give me a second chance?" Chin quivering, he gets down on his knees. "I'll come home straight from the office every day, no more drinking at the pub or workouts at the gym."

A month later ...

It is lunch break at Boon Rubber Glove Factory (name changed) and all staff are in the canteen. Or so it seems. Mr Booneung (a pseudonym), the General Manager, strolls from his office to enter the men's washroom. Standing at a urinal to release a steady stream, he hears moaning coming from one of several toilet stalls in a row. *Huh? What's going on?* Mr Booneung zippers up, goes to a spot in front of the row of cubicles. He gets down on one knee to scan below the door of each stall respectively. Inside the last stall, he spots two pairs of legs.

Mr Booneung stands up, raps the door with his knuckles and hollers, "Who's in there? Come out now! I am Mr Booneung!"

The door opens to reveal two men crammed inside, their shocked faces twisted in a grimace. *Oh Lord Buddha! Akara Karnthip, my production supervisor and Udom Songthem, my sales executive!* "What are both of you doing inside?" Mr Booneung eyes shoot daggers that can strewn bodies on the floor. "Come! Let's go to my office now!" He strides away in a huff.

Two weeks later ...
Togged up in pumps and a sheath dress, Kwanjai stands at the doorway as the wooden door is pulled open to reveal a mid-fifties woman standing behind an iron grille door. The latter is garbed in a tunic and wearing salt-and-pepper hair in a bun.

Kwanjai bows. "*Sawakee-kah*, are you the mother of Udom Songthem?"

"Yes, I am." Mrs Songthem raises her eyebrows in question. "How can I help you?"

"I am Mrs Kwanjai Karnthip. Can we talk?"

"What's it regarding?"

"My husband Akara and your son Udom."

"Oh? Come on in, please." Mrs Songthem unlocks the grille door and opens it.

Kwanjai kicks off her shoes, leaves them outside and goes to sit on the settee. Wind from an overhead pirouetting fan is grabbing the aroma of cooking from the kitchen and swirling it in the hall.

Mrs Songthem locks the grille door and goes park herself opposite Kwanjai. "Yes, what is it regarding my son?"

"First, do you know that your son is gay?"

"My husband and I've been aware of our son's sexuality since he was a teenager. My husband has tried to change him but without success. So, we've learned to accept what he is."

"My husband, Akara, and your son are lovers. I caught them in a love motel two months ago. At that time, I didn't know they're colleagues. Akara said he would try to change and become straight. Last week, Akara and Udom were caught by their employer having sex in the office toilet." Kwanjai's shoulders sag as she pins her gaze on Mrs Songthem. "They were dismissed from their jobs."

"Oh dear! Udom told me he resigned instead. How do you know all this?"

"After Akara was sacked, he told me a cock-and-bull story, but I didn't believe him, so I went to see his former employer. He told me everything. One of their ex-colleagues – he's probably a closet gay himself – gave me your address. My husband says he's still trying to change but he needs time. We are trying to save our marriage, Mrs Songthem. But, Udom must play a role by not contacting him anymore." Kwanjai's tone of voice softens to a husky plea.

"I'm so sorry. I didn't know he is involved with a married man. As a woman, I understand how you feel. I'll talk to my son."

"Thank you for your understanding, Mrs Songthem." Relief

curves Kwanjai's mouth into a gentle smile.

Mrs Songthem pulls out her mobile phone from her pants side pocket. "Son, I want you to listen to a song – it's titled If Loving You is Wrong." She taps a few buttons on her phone and places it beside her plate on the dining table. "It was a popular R&B in the nineteen seventies – you weren't even born yet."

Luther Ingram's voice sings, *"If loving you is wrong I don't wanna be right. If being right means being without you, I'd rather live a wrong doing life. Your mama and daddy say it's a shame. It's a downright disgrace. Long as I got you by my side I don't care what your people say ... Your friends tell you there's no future ...In loving a married man ..."*

The Songthem family is eating dinner in their apartment two days after Kwanjai's visit.

Udom's face turns pale. *"Mae*, what're you trying to tell me?"

Mrs Songthem taps a button on her phone to stop the audio. "Son, your boyfriend's wife came to see me. Your father and I can accept your sexuality, but we cannot condone you breaking up someone's marriage." She replaces the phone back in her side pocket. "Please leave Akara and find someone who's single and unattached."

Between bites of rice Sirichai Songthem adds, "Love can drive a man to ecstasy, misery, victory, disappointment, desperate chances and broken rules. Don't break the rules, son."

Six months pass ...

Udom enters a cubicle in the men's washroom and flips the lid of the toilet bowl down. He sits on the lid, takes out his mobile phone and dials his ex-colleague's number. "Hello Artichart?

How're things at the Boon factory? Hmmm … I see. I'm fine in my new job. Actually, I called you regarding Akara. I heard from Warinton that Akara and his wife are divorced. You know where he is now?"

"Yes. He's in Surat Thani Town. Chai and I visited him last month, part-visit and part-holiday in Koh Samui."

"Can you give me his contact number?"

"Sorry, I can't. He made us promise that we won't let anyone have his contact number." A pause. "Sorry to say this, but he wants to be left alone. Why don't you forget him and move on?"

"Come on, please. My love for him is too strong to let him go just like that. He broke off with me without saying anything."

"Sorry, buddy, a promise to him is a promise."

"Tell you what. Take me to see him instead. In that way, you won't be breaking your promise to him, right? I'll pay for the bus fare and one night's hotel accommodation." Udom blasts out a sigh. "I can only forget Akara when he tells me to leave him straight in my face."

"You'll regret the trip there. It'll be a waste of time and money."

"Please …help me come to terms with whatever the reality is."

"Hmmm … alright. But don't tell me I didn't warn you."

"Thank you." He rises, pulls the lever of the cistern and a cascade of water splashes under the lid.

Surat Thani Town …
Sunrise, pinkish in glow, spreads over the roofs of buildings to herald a new day, chasing away grey mists. Udom and Arthichart – both togged up in t-shirts and slacks – are traipsing down a tree-

lined drag where only a few pedestrians are out and about.

Udom flicks a side glance at Arthichart and back at the drag ahead. "Where are you taking me?"

"Just follow me if you want to meet Akara."

Artichart stops outside the entrance of a small temple and checks his watch. "We'll wait here."

"You've arranged for Akara for meet us here?"

Artichart does not answer and gazes past Udom with a faraway look in his eyes.

Ten minutes pass. Four robe-clad monks plod on their bare feet in a single file out of the entrance gate in their morning routine to collect food.

Udom's widened eyes gobble up the scene. Shock sways his shoulders as he sways on his feet. The first monk is Akara! Udom clamps a steadying hand on Artichart's shoulder as the former's head stirs in a dizzy swirl.

Sporting a bald head, Akara darts his gaze at Artichart and Udom, ignores them with a stony expression and continues his way in silence.

Back to the present ...

"I was devastated, got depressed and couldn't concentrate on my work. In the end, I decided I needed a new environment to start afresh. That's why I came to Phuket. I'm meeting lots of men here and am happy in my job." Udom flicks his gaze at my beer stein. "You want another beer?"

"Why, sure!" I nod. "You want another man-whore drink?

Kuala Lumpur Medley

Charles tosses his gaze from the hostesses parading on the stage to me. "The Hong Kong style knock-knock system is here in Malaysia." He has sharp, pinched features and wears his hair slicked back.

"Oh?" I turn my head to return a smile at the mamasan walking past our table and look back to Charles. "How does that work?"

"You knock on the door, enter the room, view the working lady, ask her price and decide whether you want to take her or not." Charles lifts his stein to his lips. "That system is popular in Hong Kong." Throat glugging, he upends the stein until the beer is gone and replaces it in its former spot.

"Which part of KL?"

"Not in KL, in Klang." Charles snaps his fingers at a passing flower-girl. "I'll text the hotel's name and address to you."

Carrying several garlands in the crook of her arm, the flower-girl stops at our table. Charles chooses a garland, puts it on top of the table and pays the girl who goes away.

"How to know which room's door to knock?"

Charles leans sideways and cranes his neck to get a better view of the hostesses on the stage. "The whole floor is dedicated to working ladies." He whisks his gaze back to me. "Look under the door. Light on means she is available, light off means she's working. There're no pimps around but they're observing you through CCTVs. So, watch your behaviour." Charles rises from his chair and grabs his garland. "Excuse me, buddy, I want to collar a girl." He runs a hand over his hair at the back of his head.

The lift I am standing in jolts to a halt and its twin doors slide apart. I step into the musky corridor and turn right to start my search for an interviewee. I cast my gaze down at the bottom of the first door at the left. The lights are switched off and I move a step closer to the door. My jaw drops! Muffled moaning is coming through the door and the bed is thumping against one wall.

I walk ahead. The bottom of the next door is lighted. Inhaling a fortifying breath, I knock trice on the door with my knuckles. There is no reply. I knock again, grab the knob and turn it. The door is not locked. I swing the door inward and step inside the room.   An oval-faced China doll, probably late twenties, is leaning against the headboard of a bed and watching a wall-mounted TV. A see-through lingerie clings to her slender body and her cream-coloured slender legs are stretched out, her toes of one leg wriggling. A newspaper is spread on her lap and it contains a pile of black pumpkin seeds. In the midst of cracking a pumpkin seed, she tosses her gaze at me, her curious small eyes bolting wider.

"*Ni hao*!" My lips upturn in a smile. "*Wo keyi caifang ni ma*? [Can I interview you?]"

"*Tiew nia ma chow hai*! I'm not interested!" Puckering her crimson lips, she spits the shells of a pumpkin seed in my direction. "Get lost!" The shells land on the floor about two feet away from me.

"Huh?" Heat sears my cheeks. "You speak Cantonese?"

"I'm from Guangzhou! Get out!" She picks up a pumpkin seed with her thumb and forefinger and tosses it at me. "Close the door!" The pumpkin seed hits my chest and falls to the floor.

Sheesh! This woman must be a veteran in this line of work. I exit her room and go to the next room. Inside, a petite China doll declines to be interviewed. Aw ... at least she isn't rude to me. I try my luck at another room on my right. A middle-aged working lady inside the room rejects my request with a smile and a gentle shake of her head. I proceed ahead and a door swings open on my right. A twenty-something man wearing Adolf Hitler-style haircut skulks out of the room with a grimace on his face, leaving the door ajar.

"Take back your money!" hollers a shrill voice from the room. "I don't do that disgusting thing!"

A wad of money notes flies out of the doorway, hitting the young john-to-be on the back of the head! The woman inside the room slams the door shut with a thud which echoes in the corridor. The red-faced man picks up the money and skedaddles to the lift lobby.

After six more futile attempts to secure an interview, I take my leave.

***

Hassan (not his real name), a burger seller, enters his sister's room with a box of Kleenex tissue in one hand. He plops the box on the dresser table and takes three steps to the closet. Sucking in a noisy inhale, he stands in front of the closet and opens the door. From a clothes hanger, he slips an A-line sleeveless dress off its metal hanger and tosses it on the nearby bed. He squats, pulls open a drawer and takes out a black E-cup brassier and a pair of black panties. He goes to the dresser, stands facing the mirror – sees a mid-twenties man with touches of humour around the mouth and near the eyes in the reflection – and strips, tossing his clothes on the floor. He puts on the brassier and steps into the panties. From the box of Kleenex tissue, he pulls out several plies and wads them. He fills up the cups of the bra with the wadded tissue papers, takes a stick of lipstick from the dresser top and paints his lips red. Then he moves to the bed, picks up the dress and puts it on. From a hook on one wall, he takes a strap handbag and hangs it over one shoulder. He exits his sister's room and deposits his own clothes in his own room. Then he crosses the hall where his father is sitting on an armchair, reading a newspaper.

"*Ayah* [Father], I am going out to run the errands now."

His wizened father looks up from his newspaper. "Okay." His voice is a near growl. The oldster picks up a sheaf of papers from the coffee table and hands it over. "Do as I tell you, okay?"

Hassan nods and takes the sheaf of papers. At the doorway, he takes a pair of his sister's kitten heel shoes and straps them on. He opens the gate, climbs on his motorcycle and rides off.

Inside a post office, Hassan jabs at a button on the ticket machine which spits out a paper with a number. He takes the paper and grabs a seat in the waiting area. From the corner of his eyes, he sees two women seated nearby staring at him. Hassan cringes in embarrassment. The LED screen of the call system dings and his number appears. He steps to the counter, opens his handbag and takes out the electricity and phone bills. The female clerk clamps her mouth in a straight line to stifle a snigger. *Puki-mak! This is so embarrassing.* Hassan looks away from her.

Inside a supermarket, Hassan pushes a trolley along a corridor between display shelves to search for items on the shopping list given by his father. Carrying a basket in one hand, a young man, browsing a row of canned food snags his gaze at Hassan. The young man meanders his gaze at Hassan from his stubbly face to his bulging chest to his hairy legs protruding from the hem of his skirt. The former mocks a shudder, grins a half-smile and continues to browse. *Dammit! I'm a laughing stock!* Hassan takes three packets from the shelf and starts to proceed to the cashier's counter. *Shit! Afterwards, I've to eat lunch at Kassim Nasi Kandar Restaurant and bring the receipt home. That place is packed with people.* Heat circles his collar.

As the sun descends over the city roofline, Hassan rides his motorcycle to his burger stall at the roadside in front of a convenience store in Chow Kit district. He stops at the stall and parks it in the walkway. His partner, Zainal, is sitting at a table and peeling off the skin of cucumbers. Zainal looks up from the cucumber in his hand to Hassan as he approaches and the former's jaw drops. "My goodness! Why're you wearing women's clothes? Have you gone bonkers?"

"I'll tell you the story later." Hassan removes his helmet, steps to his stall and opens a door at its bottom cabinet. He keeps the helmet inside and takes out bags of buns, packets of waxed paper, a griddle and squirt bottles of sauce. As he is moving a gas cylinder to the side of his stall, he hears a bleat of a horn. His father is astride his Yamaha Lagenda, its engine sputtering. Eyes glinting like molten steel, his father nods and rides away.

Four hours pass. A gang of four bikers clad in faux leather jackets stop at the stall. They switch off the engines of their machines but remain sitting with legs astride. One of them gets off his bike, steps up to Hassan and say, "F-four beef burgers –" he releases a guffaw and doubles up with laughter " – w-without mayonnaise!" Hassan slips four pieces of beef burgers on the griddle and Zainal takes out four buns from a plastic bag and starts to slice them into halves. The four youths step a few feet away and talk among themselves. Hassan overhears one of them say, "What a laugh! This is the first time, I've seen a *pondan* [ladyboy] selling burgers!"

Minutes later, the four bikers ride off with their burgers. Shaking his head, Zainal says to Hassan, "Buddy, can you tell me why you're in drag, tonight?"

One day earlier …
Sitting on the edge of his bed, Hassan yaps on his mobile phone, "Last weekend, it was hilarious! We picked up a *pondan*. Oh … Near Wisma Masjid India, after mid-night … Yes …The *pondan* rode pillion on Yazid's bike to a park. I followed behind. When we got down, I pulled off the ladyboy's wig!" He chortles and slaps his knees. "More to come. Then we tore off his blouse and –"

"Hassan!" His father's voice blasts in the doorway. Dammit! He forgot to close the door!

Ayah steps into the room. "What did you do? You harassed a transgender?" He brandishes a finger in Hassan's face. "Transgender people are born that way! Leave them alone! Do you know their difficulties due to discrimination by society?"

"I'm sorry, *Ayah*!"

"Sorry is not good enough. I want you to be in the shoes of a transgender for a day. Then only you will empathize with them." *Ayah*'s salt-and-pepper moustache twitches at one side.

"Tomorrow, I want you to dress up in your sister's clothes and pay the utilities bill for me, then pick up a few things from the supermarket. After that, take your lunch at Kassim Nasi Kandar Restaurant. Bring the receipt back to me as proof. In the evening, run your burger stall in drag." Raising his grey beetle eyebrows, *Ayah* grinds his jaw. "Don't change clothes in a public toilet. I'll be coming to the stall to check on you."

Hassan stares at his father, mouth ajar for a moment. "B-but, that embarrassing. "I won't do it – I mean, I can't do it."

"If you don't do what I say, I'll stop paying your motorbike instalments from next month onward." *Ayah* turns on his heels and leaves the room.

***

The lift glides to a halt and its doors slide open. Inside the lift, Andrew Au (a pseudonym), mid-twenties, picks up his aluminum toolbox and steps out into the corridor. He turns left and saunters past two apartments. *Hmmm ... the numbers are getting bigger. Should be the other direction.* He pivots on one heel, turns, and strides ahead. He finds the apartment he's looking for, rings the doorbell and waits.

The wooden door swings to open to reveal a bombshell, garbed in a tank top and a pair of running shorts, standing behind the grille door. "Are you Andrew?" She flutters her eyelashes as air-conditioned gusts escape from inside the apartment to fight with the warm air in the corridor.

"Yes, I am." A grin parts Andrew's lips, revealing a flash of teeth.

The sex bomb jiggles the bunch of keys in her hand, finds the right one and unlocks the grille door. Andrew steps inside and she re-locks the grille door and slams the wooden door shut.

"Girls, Andrew's here," announces the sex kitten as she gestures Andrew to one of two chairs stationed near the glass sliding door of the balcony. "Who wants to be first?"

"Xiao-Ling, you go ahead," says a melodious voice from the kitchen. "I'll be out soon, after I finish this dish."

"I'll be last," comes another voice from a bedroom.

Xiao-Ling sits with her back facing Andrew who stoops to rest his aluminum tool box on its side and opens the lid. Inside the box are scissors, curling tools, shampoos and styling products.

He whips out a plastic file folder and hands it to Xiao-Ling. "Which hair style do you want?"

Xiao-Ling takes the folder containing photos of different hair styles, flicks through several pages and stops at a particular page. "This one!" She points a dainty finger with varnished nail at a photograph.

Andrew looks over the shoulder of Xiao-Ling. "Aaah, a long bob with waves." His gaze skitters to her breasts, the full curving roundness of them straining against the fabric of her tight top. "It's perfect for your face. Easy to maintain too."

"Can I see the photo book?" asks a low voice, velvet-edged and clear.

Andrew turns towards the source of the voice. A tall twenty-something lass with long shapely legs and a curvy frame has one arm stretched out to receive the folder file from Xiao-Ling. *Wow! I wonder how those legs would feel wrapped around my waist!* From the back of the apartment, enters a petite girl togged up in a mini gym shorts barely long enough to cover the swell of her butt and a cropped top that reveals a dangerous amount of cleavage.

Andrew's jaw drops as he picks up a pair of thinning scissors to work on Xiao-Ling's hair. *Phew! Lucky, I wanked before coming here.*

Almost two hours later, after having styled the three girls' hair, Andrew jabs the doorbell of the adjacent apartment. A Vietnamese girl whose hips taper into long straight legs lets him inside where three other babes, in the midst of watching TV, turn to eyeball him.

Back to the present ...
Andrew grips several strands of noodles with a pair of chopsticks. "In one afternoon, I styled the hair of seven girls, all nightclub hostesses." He lifts the noodles to his mouth and starts to eat.

"Wow!" I spear a dumpling with a fork and sink a bite into it. "How did you manage to penetrate that market?"

Andrew looks around the coffee shop to make sure no one is eavesdropping. "I met up with the mamasan." He licks his lips. "I offered her a commission and a free haircut. Also, I told her I'll be visiting her nightclub. So, what I earn from the haircut will in part go back to her."

***

Clove cigarette clamped between his teeth, Kristiono is cruising on a motorbike along a deserted drag in Kuala Lumpur's Chow Kit district. Riding pillion behind, Darma is observing the shuttered stores on the left.

In their mid-twenties, Darma and Kristiono arrived illegally by boat from Java, Indonesia, two months ago. They hold day jobs as food-stall helpers and commit petty thefts at night.

As the motorcycle passes the empty parking lot of a cinema, Darma taps Kristiono on the shoulder. "Slow down, someone's inside a car parked in there. I can see the glow of a cigarette butt."

Kristiono turns his head and says, "I'll switch off the lights, make a loop and we'll go on foot for a closer look."

He rounds the cinema with lights switched off and stops in the shadows of an adjacent building. The duo gets off and walk half-crouched across the deserted road to enter the parking lot. They steal to a spot about fifteen feet away from the car and squat.

"Do you see her?" Darma half-whispers. "Looks like a long-haired woman in the passenger seat."

"Yesus! The hooker's giving the little man in the driver's seat a blowjob!" Kristono reaches for a penknife in his jeans back pocket. "See her head bobbing up and down?"

"Yup, they're easy targets! Let's rob them!" Darma pulls out a kitchen knife wrapped in an old newspaper from under his belt. "You take the woman; I take the man." He unwraps the kitchen knife and drops the newspaper to the ground.

Kristono darts to the side of the passenger seat, holding his penknife aloft. "Gimme your handbag! This is a stickup!"

The long-haired woman turns sideways and flings the door open, slamming it at Kristono, who staggers backward. She then steps out of the car to reveal her enormous frame togged up in jeans and a top and delivers a kick to Kristono's chest. "Haaaaiiiiyaaah!" Her voice is like a bear's growl.

"Shit!" Eyes widened in shock, Kristono falls on his butt and drops his penknife. "She's a ladyboy! And over six feet tall!" He scrambles up on his bare feet, his slippers having slipped off. "Run, Darma! Run! Run!"

The duo scurries back to their motorcycle.

***

Chinatown, Kuala Lumpur, a year ago ...

Leaning on a Malacca cane walking stick, seventy-year-old Ah-Fook moves with a shuffling gait to the living room where his youngest son is lounging on a faux leather settee and fiddling a portable video games console.

Jeffrey (not his real name), aged twenty-six, looks up from the console in his hands. "Yes, Papa?" He puts the console on his lap and sits straighter.

Ah-Fook plops his frail frame down beside Jeffery, leans the walking stick against the settee and locks his eyes on his son in a serious gaze. "Son, I've something to tell you." He starts to cough but holds it in.

"What about, Papa?"

"This afternoon, I went to the hospital. The doctor said my lung cancer is now in stage two." His wrinkly face crumples as he mops a gnarled hand over it. "It's time for me to meet my Maker soon. So, I've decided to bequeath my piles clinic to you."

"Papa, I'm content to continue as a delivery-man in Uncle's furniture store." *WTF! How am I going to get a girlfriend as a piles traditional doctor?*

"Haven't you heard? Your uncle's closing the shop down next year. He wants to retire. I guess, he hasn't told you yet." Ah-Fook starts to cough again. "Tomorrow, I'm going to start training you –" he puts his right hand to his mouth to block the cough " – how to treat piles the traditional way."

"But –"

Ah-Fook takes his gnarled hand away. "Be proud of our family tradition, son." He looks at his palm.

"Oh, my God! There's blood on your hand!" A pang of guilt seizes Jeffrey. "Alright, Papa, whatever you say."

Kuala Lumpur, a year ago ...
"Papa," asks Ken, "what did the heart doctor say?" He shovels a spoonful of rice into his mouth.

Old Sung shakes his head and pushes his empty plate aside. "No good, son. My heart disease is worsening."

Mrs Sung unscrews the cap of a bottle of pills and pours one out. From a second bottle, she shakes out a capsule. "Here, take your medications, dear."

The Sung family is eating dinner in their apartment, one floor above their coffin shop in Sungei Besi district.

Old Sung pops the pills into his mouth and washes them down with a gulp of Chinese tea. "Ken, I want you to quit your job, take over the funeral business. I'll teach you how to handle the duties of a funeral director."

"But, Papa, I'm happy in my job." *Shit! I don't want to be a coffin seller! Which girl will see me as a potential husband material? A* lump rises in Ken's throat.

"I built up this business from scratch, and it took me a lifetime. You grew up among coffins, literally. When you and your siblings were kids, you used to play hide-and-seek in the shop, hiding in empty coffins. I don't want to see my efforts go down the drain when I'm gone."

Mrs Sung chips in, "Be obedient, son, submit your resignation letter tomorrow."

"Yes, Papa."

Back to the present …

Jeffrey takes a gulp of his beer and puts the mug down. "I wasn't a piles traditional doctor for long. "That line of work did not give me job satisfaction."

Seated beside Jeffrey, Ken adds, "I ran my late father's coffin shop for about a year. Then I met Jeffrey and we decided to open this bar. So, I sold off the coffin shop. That's how we became business partners."

I flick my gaze sideways to bob-haired Mummy Josephine, probably in her early thirties, sitting beside me. "What were you doing before you joined this bar?"

"I was a make-up artist." Mummy spears a piece of pineapple from a platter and brings it to her mouth. "But I wasn't happy with my job."

I take a sip of my Bloody Mary through a straw in the glass. "Why?"

Mummy says with her mouth full, "I had difficulty finding a boyfriend because of my job."

"Oh?" I stir my Bloody Mary with the plastic swizzle. "What's wrong with being a make-up artist?"

"I was a make-up artist for the dead."

My jaw goes slack.

* * *

Sales manager Simon, early thirties in age, strides down the door showroom with Mr Quek (not his real name) following behind. Several wooden doors and security doors are mounted on mock metal doorways running parallel to one wall. Wearing a red neck-tie, Simon stops at a shiny metal door and turns to face his prospective client, a portly man in his forties.

"Mr Quek, this is our top-of-the-line security door." Simon points a finger at a shiny door. "This is made in Germany." He forms a gap between his thumb and forefinger. "It's two inches of solid steel. The lock uses a lever-and-mortise mechanism. See the keyhole? Its special design restricts access so even a professional locksmith will find it difficult to manipulate the pins inside."

He delivers a taekwondo-like kick at the door. "See? See how solid it is?" He thrusts an open palm at the door. "Try kicking it, Mr Quek. Test it."

Mr Quek kicks at the door repeatedly until his loafer flies off his foot. "Yes, it's really solid." He picks up his shoe and slips it on.

Simon steps to the next door. "This is an Italian-made door, our premium product. Its thickness is two inches of solid tungsten. In terms of tensile strength, tungsten is the hardest metal on earth – its strength is 1,500 Megapascals." He unlocks the door and swings it open. "See? The mortise lock has four individual bolts. Can you imagine how difficult to saw through the four bolts? The unique design of the faceplate also restricts access to the internal lock mechanism."

Mr Quek scratches the back of his balding head. "How much is this tungsten door?"

"Fifteen thousand, includes delivery and installation within KL."

"I want two for my brothels, err, I mean, executive spas."

Simon maintains a stoic expression. "I understand your needs, Mr Quek." He straightens his tie with both hands. "It will take the cops at least half-an-hour to break down this door."

"That's what I want." Mr Quek shows a thumbs-up. "By that

time, my girls would have escaped through a secret passage to the next building."

***

Sitting on her bed set at a wall under a first-floor window looking out to Kalong Road, Mei-San (not her real name) looks at the drag below, illuminated by street lamps. Sex workers are intermittently walking with their johns from the back entrance of One-Stop Food Court across the drag to their nearby apartments, which are shared by three or four women in the same profession. Three tough-looking bouncers are lounging on chairs under the stars, and the back entrance of the food court is jettisoning loud music.

Aged twenty-eight, Mei-San has a perfect oval face with a strong chin of determination. Clutching a spare pillow at her chest, she ponders on her present with a weary sigh. Daughter of a noodle hawker stationed in a coffee shop in Loke Yew Road, she wakes up at 5:30 am, and after breakfast at home, follows her father on his motorbike to his noodle stall. By 7 am, the stall begins for business. Business ends at 3 pm and the washing up of plates, bowls and cutlery starts. By 5 pm, she and her father are back home from the day's drudgery, tired to the bone.

Mei-San notices a long-haired China doll dressed in a bare-back halter dress strutting on heels across the drag with a paunchy client behind. *Wow! That's her fourth customer tonight.* She flicks a gaze at the alarm clock atop her battered bureau cabinet at the other side of the room. *It's only 10 pm.* Another two hours pass as if on wings. *Holy cow! That's her again! She into her sixth customer thus far.* Mentally, Mei-San reckons the amount the hooker makes per month. *By 3 am, when she stops work, probably, she would have snared a total of eight customers. Multiply that by one hundred ringgit by twenty working days, and she earns – holy cow! – sixteen thousand per month! On bad days, assume she gets only five customers per night, yet she still rakes in ten thousand a month! If I can earn that amount for three years, I'd saved enough to open a flower shop.* Her eyes grow sleepy and she unties the rubber band holding her hair in a ponytail and throws it to the floor. She closes the louvre glass window panes halfway, draws the curtains and flops backward on her bed.

Macau, two months later …

Togged up in a floral romper dress and black stockings, Mei-San enters the lounge of Queensbay Hotel & Casino (not its real name), Macau, and strolls to the acrylic bar counter, illuminated by uplights. She hitches the strap of her handbag higher up and takes small steps on stilettos parallel to the bar to assess the drinkers seated on high stools. After passing three balding men, she stops as two younger men grab her attention. *Ah! These two men are well-dressed.* She sidles up to the space between two early-thirties Chinese men – one skinny, another beefy – who're chatting in between sips of cocktails.

"Hello," Mei-San says, casting her gaze left and right. "where are you gentlemen from?"

Mr Beefy jerks his head sideways. "We're from Hong Kong." He has a firm mouth curled as if on the edge of laughter.

Mei-San runs a hand through her hair hanging in graceful curves over her shoulders. "Would you like to buy me a drink?"

Mr Skinny – wearing mop hairstyle – swivels on his stool to face Mei-San. "Of course, darling!"

Mr. Beefy leans sideways and wraps an arm around Mei-San's slender waist. "Come drink in our room. We stay in this hotel."

"You want short time or long time?"

Mr Skinny pats Mei-San's butt. "We want your asshole."

"Huh? I don't do anal sex."

Mr Beefy chortles, lips curling up. "My friend was only joking."

Mr Skinny leans towards Mei-San's private space and half-whispers, "How about a threesome?"

"Sorry, I don't do that either. One man at a time."

"But we're sharing a room."

"One of you has to wait outside."

A price for a short time is agreed.

Mr Skinny winks at Mr. Beefy. "Me first, you later."

Mei-San and Mr Skinny enters the latter's room and he closes the door and locks it. He kicks off his shoes, moves to the foot of one bed and sits on the edge of the mattress. "Can you take a shower? There are two new towels on the rack." He lifts one foot and peels off his sock. "Can I get you a drink? A soft drink, perhaps?" He tosses the sock on the bed.

"No thanks." Mei-San stretches out one hand. "Payment in advance, please."

"Oh?" Mr Skinny stands, pulls out a wallet from his side trouser pocket and extracts some money notes. He takes a few strides toward Mei-San and hands them over.

"Thank you." Mei-San slips the money notes into her handbag and enters the bathroom. A minute later, after having showered, she emerges with a bath towel wrapped around her upper torso and her hands carrying her bundled clothes and handbag. Her eyes bulge like those of a toad! A naked Mr Beefy is leaning on his back against the front door, his arms folded across his muscular chest. Mr Skinny, also in a state of nature, is waiting a few feet away from the bathroom doorway.

"Hey!" A chill runs down Mei San's spine. "I said one at a time!"

Mr Skinny darts behind Mei-San, clamps a hand over her mouth and drags her by the wrist to the nearest bed. Mr Beefy lunges forward to join Mr Skinny, and the former pushes her face down on the mattress and pins her head down on the pillow.

"No! No!" Mei-San pleads. "Please, don't!"

"Shuddup!" A big hairy fist lands on the back of her head.

Mei-San feels somebody clambering on her lower torso and something hard penetrating her butthole. "Aiiiiyaaaah!" She grits her teeth and grips at the bedsheet until her knuckles turn while.

Johor Bahru, two months later …

Mei-San enters a notorious coffee shop and grabs a table. The smell of fresh-brewed coffee and toast wafts about to loud Mandarin pop music blasting from a radio. Clustered at several tables are hordes of China dolls, some jabbering, others fiddling with their mobile phones. Prospective clients, mostly oldsters, are seated at other tables. Mei-San looks at her wrist watch. It's only 8:00 am and the flesh trade has already started. Ditto for the adjacent coffee shop, equally notorious for China-doll freelancers.

A dumpy woman dressed in frumpy clothes steps up to Mei-San's table. "Drink?"

Mei-San puts her handbag on her lap. "Black coffee."

A minute later, the dumpy woman returns with a cup of black coffee and Mei-San pays her. As Mei-San is stirring her coffee, a forty-something man rises from a corner table and saunters to her. "*Ni hao ma*?" He pulls out a chair beside Mei-san, sits and thrusts out his hand. "I'm Peter from Singapore. Are you a local?" His short-sleeved t-shirt clings to his scrawny body like it is a size too big and his dark jeans compress his crotch into a big bulge.

"Yes." Mei-San pumps his gnarled hand. "Want to come to my room?" Her eyes gleam with an alluring look. "I give massage with happy ending!"

A price is negotiated and agreed.

Five minutes later, inside a room in a nearby love motel, Peter is lying naked on a bed and Mei-San – clad only in her undies – is slapping his scrawny back with flat open palms, producing *piak! piak! piak!* which echo in the room. After a while, loud thumping rattles the front door and the knob jolts as if someone is trying to open it.

Mei-San stops her massage and swings her gaze at the door while Peter turns face up and manoeuvres to a sitting position. She starts to stride to the door. "I better check who that is."

Mei-San unlocks the door and opens it as far as the chain lock will allow.

"Open the door, you bitch!" A woman with a low forehead and a flat nose glares at Mei-San with piercing eyes. "My husband's inside!" A blue bodycon dress stretches over her stout frame. "Open the door! Let me in!"

Mei-San releases the chain lock, swings the door open and dashes to a row of hooks on a wall. She flicks her mini skirt and blouse off the hooks and starts to put them on.

Wifey darts to the side of the bed. "You rascal!" He brandishes a stout finger in Peter's face which has turned ashen. "Every weekend, you come to JB for sex, eh?"

"H-How you know where I am?"

"I discreetly installed a GPS tracker in your mobile phone!"

Wifey lunges forward and grabs Peter in a side headlock! Mei-San's jaw drops! Amidst the screams of Peter as wifey applies the pressure on the headlock, her forearm muscles bulging with the effort, Mei-San bolts bare-footed from the room, her hand carrying her stilettos.

Back to the present …

I flick my gaze from the female DJ prancing behind a console, her breasts bouncing up and down, to Mei-San sitting beside me. "How long were you in Macau?"

"One month – tourist visa." Mei-San looks at her lap and fingers the hem of her miniskirt. "Then I was in Johor Bahru." She sweeps her fake eyelashes upward. "Believe me when I say that the money is easy for a freelancer but it's not an easy life. I've met all kinds of men, from the violent to the hen-pecked. Some were nice to me; others were horrible." She grabs a Carlsberg bottle and pours more beer into my stein. "That's why I came back to work as a hostess." She plunks the beer bottle back in its former spot. "Here, we have bouncers and a mamasan to take care of us."

"What's the name of that coffee shop in Johor Bahru?"

"I don't know but it's at Meldrum Road. There're two coffee shops adjacent to each other, just next to the Merlin Tower. They are packed with freelancers, mostly from China. Many of the customers are from Singapore. The overhead link bridge connecting Merlin Tower to City Square also has working ladies hanging around." Mei-San picks up her shot glass, tosses the tequila down her throat and slams the glass down. "Hey, I've been talking to you for a long time. Can you buy a flower for me?"

"Sure!" I look around, squinting in the dim light. "Where's the flower-girl?"

"There she is!" Mei-San raises one arm and flaps her hand.

A lanky girl with a flat chest comes to our table with an assortment of garlands in one hand. "You want flower, sir?" A money pouch is strapped around her waist.

"Gimme a big garland." I shift my hip sideways to fish out my wallet from my trouser pocket. Money and garland exchange hands.

I pass the garland to Mei-San who hangs it over her neck with pride, her face beaming with glee. "Oooooh," she coos, "thank you darling!" Later, she will redeem it for cash, with a small cut going to the nightclub.

"You're welcome." I nudge my stein away with one palm. "Let's continue talking." I rest both arms on the table. "What, in your opinion, is the ideal night-clubber?"

Mei-San ponders for a moment. "The ideal night-clubber is young, late twenties or thirties, doesn't have a pineapple face, doesn't wear a moustache, dresses smartly, can dance, can crack jokes, laughs at jokes, likes to play dice games or card games – who loses kisses him; if he loses, he pays a fine – spends money like Jho Low, can interact with all levels of the staff – from bouncers to band members to DJs to hostesses to mamasans – and doesn't check his mobile phone for missed calls from wife."

My mobile phone in my pouch case hooked at my belt vibrates. I ignore it, grab my willibecher and take a long swallow of beer. My mobile phone vibrates again. I plunk my willibecher back on the coaster. I fish out my phone and look at the screen.

Great balls of fire! Two missed calls from my wifey.

***

Carrying a plastic box in one hand, Meena (not her real name) opens the door to her cubicle office and ambles two steps to her desk. She plonks down on her cushioned chair which whooshes under her weight and places the plastic box on her desk beside her computer. The aroma of vegetable curry wafts from the inside of the box as she lifts up its lid. From her left hand-side drawer, she takes out a pair of fork and spoon and starts to eat. Through the glass-portion of the wall at her side, she sees an empty hall with rows of sewing machines, its floor littered with scraps of fabric.

Thirty-six-year-old Meena is a production supervisor in a women's undergarments factory in Kepong, Kuala Lumpur. Still single, Meena comes from a family of three daughters and one son. Her two sisters have married and moved out.

As she chews her food, she logs onto her Facebook account. Her profile photo shows a plump fangled-tooth woman wearing shoulder-length hair like a hurrah's nest. She scrolls the screen down and clicks around. *Bah! No friend requests by any Indian hunks! No comments on any of my posts!* She logs off and enters IndianFriendship.com.my (not its real name) of which she is a member and checks her in-box. *Bloody hell! No replies from the men I wrote to.* She takes a swallow of her food and releases an exhale of frustration. *I hate my parents, I hate society, I hate my job, I hate myself! Chuni-warker! I can't even get laid for free!* She finishes her food, replaces the lid on the plastic box and tosses it into the wastepaper basket under her desk. From a flask a few feet away, she takes a gulp of masala tea. Now she performs a Google search for "nude webcam Indian men" and trawls out a list of sites. She clicks on the first website but a message appears with "This site has been blocked because it contravenes the laws of the country." *Shit! Never mind, I've a VPN in my home computer, will check out these sites later.* She logs off.

Meena opens the bedroom door and sticks her head out in the hallway. Her younger brother is sitting alone in the hall watching TV. *Appa and Mama are sleeping in their room. Good!* She closes the door, locks it and goes to sit at her desk next to her bed. She switches on her computer, connects to a VPN and searches for "naked webcam Indian men" on Google. A list of websites appears and she opens the first one. Her eyes jolt wider in surprise at the sight of the half-naked men in the photo section. After browsing around, she enters another site called IndianDirtyTalk. com.id (not its real name). *Hmmm … Two-way chat via Skype. This is safe, if one party is recording, the other party is notified via a message on the screen.* From a bottom right-hand drawer, she takes out a pair of headphones with a built-in mike and connects it to her computer. Then she puts on the headphones and, after several clicks of the mouse, joins as a member of the website and buys 100 tokens using her credit card.

In the photo gallery, she clicks on the image of "Ranbir", one of several male models online at the moment and her Skype call is connected to him. A twentyish man with strong facial features that hold a certain sensuality appears on her Skype screen. He is garbed in a short-sleeved checked shirt with two buttons undone, exposing a muscular hairy chest. The shadow of his beard accentuates his manly aura.

"Hello, darling, I'm Ranbir of Mumbai!" Ranbir's lips part

in a dazzling display of straight, white teeth. "I can only see part of your face."

Meena adjusts the position of her external webcam. "Can you see me now?"

"Yes, love, I can see you fully now. You're soooo ...beautiful!"

A part of Meena revels in his open admiration of her and a warm glow flows through her heart.

"What's your name, darling?"

"I'm Meena, residing in Kuala Lumpur."

After more sugary words, Ranbir asks, "How do you want me to perform?"

"I want dirty pillow talk and a strip-tease to, err, to show me your, err –"

"My twelve-inch tool? Darling, don't be shy." Ranbir's eyes blaze with passion. "That's what I'm here for – to satisfy your every fantasy, your every wish and your every command." He moves his face closer to the camera and puckers his thick lips. "Darling, hold me, thrill me and kiss me!"

The sound of Ranbir smacking his lips sends a tingle to Meena's crotch! *My God! No man has ever lusted for me, no man has ever wanted me before! And he's so young, so handsome ... He makes feel like I'm in a princess in paradise ...*

Thirty-five minutes pass. Now, Meena is staring wide-eyed at a naked Ranbir posing in the front lateral spread. Suddenly, she realises there is a stickiness between her legs. *Goodness gracious! My panties are wet!* She licks her lips, leaving them shiny and wet and slips one hand inside her panties to finger herself.

"Oooooh, darling, show me your pussy, please ..." Ranbir thrusts his hips repeatedly, his testicles swinging from side to side, and grunts "I'm sexy, baby! I'm sexy, baby!" in synchrony with each thrust. He blows out an exhale. "Come, let's have virtual sex ... Daaaarling, I worship every part of your body ..."

Meena scrutinises her Skype screen. *There is no banner to indicate he's recording.*

She leans back in her chair, pulls down her panties and spreads her legs, exposing her girl-parts to the webcam. "You like my pussy, dear?"

"Yeeeees! It's soooo ...kissable!" Ranbir's eyes bulge in their sockets. "Let's masturbate together ... let's come together ... Just imagine I'm in front of you in the flesh and blood ..."

Meena closes her eyes and masturbates, her girl-parts dripping juices, her mouth salivating at one corner, her tongue polishing gums and teeth, her throat releasing groans, her heart glowing with happiness and her common sense snuffed out by feminine lust.

The second hand of her alarm clock atop her side table completes several turns.

Thomp! Thomp! Thomp! Loud raps sound on the bedroom door.

Meena jerks out of her reverie. "Ranbir, I've gotta go! We chat again tomorrow!"

In a flurry of mouse clicks, she logs out of IndianDirtyTalk. com.id and out of Skype. She springs to her feet, creaking the chair as her weight leaves it, pulls up her panties and hitches the hem of her dress down.

She strides to the door, unlocks it and yanks it open a crack. Her mother's wrinkly face appears in the gap. "Yes, Mama?"

Mama squints her sleepy eyes, etched with crow's feet at the corners. "What're you doing inside? I thought I heard moaning and groaning?"

"Oh, I was watching a movie on Netflix." Meena forces a casual tone of voice. "There was a passionate love scene between the hero and heroine."

"Don't sleep too late, okay?"

"Sure, Mama." Closing the door, Meena scans her room for the tissue box.

A week later ...

In the middle of her lunch break, Meena is humming a happy tune as she logs into her account in IndianFriendship.com.my. She checks her in-box and finds it's empty. She is indifferent as over the past week, she has had three encounters with Ranbir and each ended with a climax. She is happy. Now she checks her Facebook account and sees a friend request. She clicks on it. Lo-and-behold! It's from Ranbir of Mumbai! *Holy cow! I can't believe it's him!* She accepts his friend request. Later in the evening on the same day, she and Ranbir chat briefly on Facebook Messenger.

Another two days pass ...

Insider her bedroom, Meena enters her Facebook account and sees a notification from Ranbir. She clicks on Messenger and reads the message:

> *Darling, pay me USD5,000 or I'll upload your naughty videos on YouTube. Also post them on Facebook. I've connected with your parents, siblings and friends on Facebook.*

A chill shoots down Meena's spine. *What's this? How did he record anything?*

With trembling fingers, she bashes out a reply: *Prove to me you have a video.*

Ranbir suddenly appears online and responds: *Here it is, darling, a clip.*

Meena opens the video, watches it and shock paralyzes her for a moment. *WTF! That son-of-a-bitch had a separate video camera recording the images on his computer screen. Oh my God! My face is recognizable in the video!*

Meena types: *Please, I don't have so much money*

Don't lie. You're a production manager, you have the money.

I'm only a pizza delivery girl! I lied to impress you.

I don't care what you are. Here are my Paypal details. Transfer the money to me within three days or else ...

Ranbir signs out of Facebook. Meena enters IndianDirtyTalk.com.id and makes a Skype call to him.

"Yes, darling?" Ranbir asks.

Missing is the tenderness in his eyes. Gone is the warmth in his voice. Absent is the friendliness in his expression.

"Please, don't do this to me – I don't have money."

"You'll have to find a way to get the money." Ranbir terminates the call.

Meena logs off her computer and staggers on wobbly knees to lie on her bed, her eyes fixated on the ceiling, her face perspiring, and her mind like a rat trapped in a cage and scurrying around in desperation.

Back to the present ...

Meena lifts her mug of coffee and blows at it. "Initially, I panicked but, in the end,, nothing happened." She takes a sip and puts the mug down.

I stir my cup of tea. "Did you pay him any money?"

"No, it was an empty threat, and I called his bluff." Meena leans back in her seat. "I know the social media habits of my parents, siblings and close friends. They don't accept friend requests from strangers on Facebook." She folds her arms across her ample chest. "So, on that score, I was safe. I don't know whether Ranbir uploaded my video or not but if he had, it would have been taken down quickly by the moderator." She straightens up. "I've learned a lesson – never trust any man in that profession."